THE FATHER/SON PARADIGM

Randy Boyd

DEDICATION

I would like to dedicate this book to five men who the Lord has brought across my life. The first is my natural father, Harvey Boyd. I have learned more about being a father, both natural and spiritual, from Dad than anyone else. Dad was and still is a consistent man who sincerely loves the Lord and his family above himself. He taught me to study hard, work hard, tell the truth, be loyal even if it costs you, and love Jesus. Then entered Jimmy Joe Robinson, my father-in-law. When the Lord brought Callie and me together, He gave me more than a wife; He gave me a second father. Jimmy Joe made everything fun, told everyone he met about Jesus, yet never compromised his convictions. Then in our coaching years, the heavenly Father brought another father into our lives, Buster Leaf, the head coach we served under for years. He was such a great example of a natural dad and a leader of men that I would not be the man I am today without the eight years I spent under his example. Two other men waltzed into our lives as mighty spiritual fathers, Alan Vincent, who is now in heaven with his Father, and Jack Taylor. Through these two men, I discovered the centrality of this fact, the Kingdom of God is a family led by fathers and mothers under Jesus's authority and care. Jesus, thank you for Alan and Jack; we owe so much to each of you and could never repay all you've taught us and done for us. This book is a result of these five men in our lives. Enjoy!

CONTENTS

THE CRY FOR SPIRITUAL FATHER'S TODAY

I'll never forget growing up as a little boy with a highly successful father. I came from a great home. In our early days we didn't follow Jesus too closely, but all else was right in the world of our home. My mom and dad loved each other and they loved us. They provided well for us and taught us good morals while instilling within us a love of learning. We had a great family.

Dad was a highly successful businessman in one of the most successful companies across America. He often worked long hours and was so successful that we moved to a new assignment for him about every two years. I'll always remember those times when his work required much of him and he was away. I wanted him to come home and play. I wanted Dad to throw the ball, shoot some hoops, or help me ride my new little red bike. I wanted him to read a bedtime story or tell me of his grand achievements at the office. Dad was my hero. Although his success took him away, at times perhaps more than some of the fathers of my friends, when my dad was home, he was always there for us. But during those away times, no amount of Mom telling me he would be home soon or next week would cover the cry in my little boy's heart, "I want my Dad. When will Dad be home?"

THE EARTH'S CRY

There is a cry arising from the fabric of our world today—it's the cry for fathers and mothers—those who through love and consistent input produce healthy sons and daughters! The entire earth is bellowing for deep, real relationships between the generations. Children in our homes around the world live without fathers. Can you hear them, "Daddy, where are you? I need you." Young men and women somewhat lost along life's journey are asking, "Who will help me? Who will guide me? Who will be there for me?" Even the more mature seek guidance from those who have gone before them and are finishing well. Can you hear the cry?

In America alone, 1 in 4 children (about 20 million at last count) grow up without a father in the home. The results are devastating! Fathers produce security, identity, the ability to trust, the desire for learning, and the propensity to be successful on the job. Ladies please forgive me, for I am in no way lowering the beauty and power of motherhood, but there is not a crisis of motherhood in any way comparable to fatherhood! The worldwide lack of fathers produces children who become adults who have a much greater risk of living in poverty, suffering teen pregnancy, a life that leads to some form of crime, and the list goes on. There is a cry for fathers today. Fatherlessness is one of the greatest crises on earth!

IT'S A SPIRITUAL CRY

Unfortunately within the church, there is not that great a difference. We suffer from an absence of healthy, life-giving spiritual fathers and mothers. Within the Church, who by necessity has organized herself for growth and function around practical business oriented principles, there is the cry, "Who will show me the way? How do I live for Him, get close to Him, and find His path in this spiritual walk?" We have wonderful ministries in every conceivable area within our congregational lives, but where are the fathers and mothers? Where are those who will walk beside us saying, "Let me show you the way. Follow me as I follow Christ."

Jim Wall, an apostolic leader in a church-planting movement, illustrates this void in the following story, "I didn't realize as we went to dinner that night that my life would never be the same. A few years ago, Joel Comiskey and I taught a seminar on 'cell church planting' in San Salvador, El Salvador. As we sat at dinner with several local pastors, I asked one what he considered to be the greatest need in the Salvadorian Church. He replied very solemnly, 'We are orphans. Our greatest need is spiritual fathers.' This was a man who had planted a church that had grown to 3,000+ active attendees. The church had more than 350 cell groups operating. They had launched successful daughter churches in several of the major cities of the nation. By all accounts he was highly successful. He was a spiritual father in his own rite. But there was still a void[1]."

The earth itself is crying out for fathers and sons. Listen to Paul's words, "For the creation eagerly waits with anticipation for God's sons to be revealed" (Romans 8:19 HCSB). The apostle declares that all of the created realm is standing on its tiptoes in anxious anticipation for God's sons (this word is used without gender to describe all of His children) to be revealed, but how will these sons be revealed? They will be revealed when mature fathers and mothers reach out and reach back to the younger ones longing for a guide and say, "Come on. I'll show you the way!" The Father/Son Paradigm is written into the very DNA of all of creation, and creation itself is craving the return to life-giving multigenerational relationships.

MY BEGINNINGS

When I entered the Kingdom at 15 years old, all went reasonably well until I entered university. In those early days of being away from home and trying to navigate a deeper walk with Christ while learning to make healthy life decisions, I found arising in my own heart the cry for a spiritual father. It's so hard to explain, but from the most fundamental regions of my soul, an intense longing broke forth for an older brother or father who had gone before me and would help me navigate this Kingdom way. One older gentleman came quite quickly into my life only to leave me disappointed and discouraged about the whole idea of being discipled by the next generation. Then in God's great graciousness, I met David and Ed. These two brothers really didn't know each other and at times seemed to be working at very different angles in my life, but I'll never forget that feeling of knowing that they were there. They became a part of Jesus's anchor for my soul. They became a guide to me, a sounding board for both new ideas and important decisions. As changes came about by the Holy Spirit, they comforted me and guided me into a deeper and more solid place in Christ. I am eternally grateful for these men and their role in my life.

When Callie and I were in the early days of our marriage, we met Tommy. Tommy was a pastor in a neighboring community and we often had him come and share at the Christian Club we had established on our local high school campus. Each time he came, he brought a young man with him who shared his testimony with our group prior to Tommy's riveting talks. Man, could he move you with the words of Christ! After several of these incidents of seeing a young guy share before our invited guest, I asked Tommy what was up with the young men he always brought. Tommy shared how he and his wife had decided to be a guide for the emerging servants of Jesus. They had built a couple of bedrooms on the rear of their home with a small bath and kitchen. Tommy shared how they read the Scriptures together each morning, ate often together, and "did much of life together." We had never seen anything like this but from that moment on, we were "in"! We would learn this art of becoming a spiritual father and mother the younger ones He was touching.

I am 57 years old at the time of this writing and still today, I have fathers and mentors in my life. For many years, Alan and Eileen Vincent were our teachers, our guides, our role models, and examples. Jackie and Linda White have been a guiding influence since before we were married 34 years ago. Jackie performed our wedding, brought both Callie and I into the ministry, and he was there for us when she miscarried our first child due to my foolishness. We have watched them and walked beside them as they raised their three girls. They became one of our models for a Kingdom family. Even today, Jackie serves on our board and Linda is a close friend to Callie. The Lord brought Jack and Friede Taylor into our lives 12 years ago with a lavish stroke of His hand. They waltzed in in such an unsuspecting way and have been a lighthouse to us for Kingdom living ever since! Their tireless pursuit and preaching of the Kingdom of God is more than inspirational, and the way Friede carries the Holy Spirit is so beautiful. Even as a man approaching the latter years of his journey in Christ, I need a father. I need men and women in my life who have gone before me and are a lighthouse pointing the way forward into the safe harbors of His Kingdom ways! There IS a cry for fathers today!

A BRIEF MOMENT OF CLARIFICATION

At the onset of this booklet, I want to make a few things very clear. When I speak of the Father/Son Paradigm, I am using this term with no gender specificity. I am not merely referring to a man as a father. I am also speaking of the need for mothers to rise up into their place in the Kingdom of God. When I use the word "son" I am using it in the same sense as the New Testament. In many places Paul and other New Testament writers refer to the Christian population as sons.

> "For you have not received a spirit of slavery leading to fear again, but you have received a spirit of adoption as *sons* by which we cry out, 'Abba! Father!' The Spirit Himself testifies with our spirit that *we are children of God*, . . . For the

anxious longing of the creation waits eagerly for the revealing of <u>the sons of God.</u>"

Romans 8:15–16,19 (NASB)

"But when the fullness of the time came, God sent forth His Son, born of a woman, born under the Law, so that He might redeem those who were under the Law, that we might receive <u>the adoption as sons.</u> <u>Because you are sons</u>, God has sent forth the Spirit of His Son into our hearts, crying, 'Abba! Father!'Therefore you are no longer a slave, <u>but a son;</u> and if a son, then an heir through God."

Galatians 4:4–7 (NASB)

Please forgive me the labor that it would take to speak of both a Father/Son and Mother/Daughter Paradigm. I assure you from the very beginning of this work, I am speaking about both. I am convinced by the years of travel and ministry that we simply need the older, mature, fruitful generations reaching back with an open hand and an available life to the emerging young sons and daughters bringing them into maturity and fruitful living.

But even in making this clarifying statement, I still have in my heart to speak to men. It's time for men to take their place, and specifically men of the Kingdom of God. Around the world, the greatest crises are not water shortages, food shortages, poverty, crime, or drugs. The greatest tragedy is fatherlessness! Men, rise up, reach out, and reach back to the next generation and take them along with you in this grand adventure Jesus called the Kingdom of heaven!

PACO

In Ernest Hemingway's story "The Capital of the World," we find the heartbreaking story of a Spanish father named Carlos and his alienated son, Paco. After years of a difficult relationship,

Paco finally left home, leaving a broken relationship behind. Carlos eventually discovered that Paco had gone to Madrid, and he soon followed his son there to find him and reconcile their relationship. After many frustrating days of searching, the desperate father placed an ad in the personal column of the Madrid newspaper. The father's plea read, "Dear Paco, please meet me in front of the national government building at noon. All is forgiven. I love you, Your father." Hemingway ends his story, with the father on the steps of the government all crying out into the mass of people, "Paco, I am here! Where are you?" To which 800 young men named Paco turned and replied, "I am here father," seeking to find and reconcile with their fathers.

Hemmingway strikes at a deep sickness that plagues our world—the desire and need for fathers today. How many Paco's are there in the Body of Christ worldwide seeking a relationship with a father or mother who will be a guiding influence in their journey ahead?

SMALL GROUP DISCUSSION QUESTIONS:

What need do you see in the world around us for fathers and mothers? What need do you see in the Body of Christ for fathers and mothers to take their place? What are the effects on the younger generations trying to grow without fathers and mothers to guide them? What would be the greatest results of the release of fathers and mothers in the Body of Christ?

CHAPTER TWO

THE OPERATING SYSTEM OF THE KINGDOM

This Father/Son Paradigm is written into the fabric of creation. As well as being the relational DNA code of creation, it is also the language of the Bible. Our Scriptures are full of this language and examples of this principle at work. It must be noted that the Scriptures are also full of examples of when it was lacking and the devastating results of the lack of spiritual fathers!

Spiritual parenting is the very language God has chosen to describe this incredible paradigm He desires to be a foundational principle of daily life in the Kingdom of God. If we were to list all the scriptural references, this volume would be so lengthy, all of us would exhaustedly put it aside as I labored to prove my point, but instead of that, let's look at a few of these together.

BIBLE STUDY:

Genesis 25:5–6; Numbers 27:18–23; 2 Kings 2:9–14; Malachi 4:6; John 15:11–15; 1 Corinthians 4:15; 2 Timothy 2:1–2

Read the passages above and describe the language and the practical application of these verses in regard to the Father/Son Paradigm.

MOSES AND JOSHUA

Moses found Joshua quite early in Moses's rise as the deliverer of Israel. We really don't know much of Joshua's early life, but he became known as the assistant of Moses. He served Moses, he carried out the words God gave to Moses, and he cared for the mission God had given this deliverer as if it were his own. But let's take a look at how Moses treated this young man:

- *When Moses went atop Mount Sinai to receive the covenant of the Lord from which we received the Ten Commandments, he took Joshua with him.*

- *When battles began to emerge against the inhabitants of the land along the way to the Promised Land, he asked Joshua to lead the men into battle. There is no indication that he had had any military training or experience, but Moses believed in him and empowered him as a leader.*

- *When Moses would go into the tent of meeting to encounter and hear from the Lord God Himself, he would take Joshua with him (Exodus 33:7–11). There is an interesting end to this story, "So the Lord spoke to Moses face to face, as a man speaks to his friend. And he would return to the camp, but his servant Joshua the son of Nun, a young man, did not depart from the tabernacle" (verse 11 NKJV).*

- *When Moses's time of departure came on the horizon, the Lord spoke to him to impart His Spirit of leadership upon Joshua to lead the people. It's clear this young man was like a son to this great man, and that everything Moses had, he gave to this young man who ended up doing things that Moses himself never did— get the people of Israel into the Promised Land.*

This was the Father/Son Paradigm at work!

ELIJAH AND ELISHA

As we look into the relationship of Elijah and Elisha we find a tremendous principle—the spiritual son received a double portion of the father's grace and anointing. Elijah found Elisha at a young age, and the young man began to follow the prophet. It is quite amazing how Elijah invites the youngster to be his follower, his disciple. He walks by him without saying a word and throws his mantle over the young farmer's shoulders. This throwing of the mantle upon him in the days of Elijah had a two fold meaning. First, it was Elijah saying to Elisha, "I see potential in you to be like me. Come follow me to learn the prophetic ways and enter the prophetic life." But there was a second meaning in the days of Elijah and Elisha. When someone would adopt a child that was not their own, they would place their mantle over them signifying that now you are mine and I will care for you and you shall be a son to me. We cannot be sure that this is what Elisha understood to be happening or even considered, but we do know that as Elijah was being whisked away by a fiery chariot that Elisha cried, "My father, my father, the chariots of Israel and its horsemen!" By this time in their journey together, Elisha clearly felt that Elijah was a father figure in his life and calling.

What did Elisha do when he was left there standing alone by the river as Elijah had vanished into the heavens? He picks up that same mantle that was thrown over him in adoption years before and begins to operate in a faith and power that even Elijah never displayed. His father had left him a double portion of the anointing upon his life as symbolized by the mantle, and the "son" picks it up and continues the ministry at a whole new level.

JESUS AND THE TWELVE

It is more than apparent that the great rabbi, Jesus of Nazareth, lived among His young followers as a father figure and they were like sons to Him. He was their rabbi, their teacher, their guide, their example, their corrector, their encourager, and their friend. He most perfectly revealed the Father/Son Paradigm in

His three and a half years with these young men (I say young because when they first began to follow Jesus, they were probably 15–20 years old). The greatest tool in His arsenal of preparation of these young fishermen, tax collectors, and nobodies from nowhere was time spent together. It was the master weapon in His quiver. It was the Father/Son Paradigm at work in its finest form!

PAUL AND TIMOTHY

Many times in the writings of Paul to young Timothy, you see the elder statesman use the term, "my true son in the faith." His two letters to the young man are personal, heartfelt, and low on doctrinal inspiration, but high on fatherly advice. Paul saw this young man as his closest disciple and it was a relationship that shared deep affection and genuine, heartfelt concern. The practicality and warmth of these two epistles are very moving and can only be fully understood in light of an older follower of Christ giving deep advice and coaching to a young man whom he knew well and loved dearly. In these two letters, we see this Father/Son Paradigm at work. Listen to Paul to Timothy and about Timothy:

> *"Paul, an apostle of Christ Jesus by command of God our Savior and of Christ Jesus our hope, To Timothy, my true child in the faith."*
>
> *1 Timothy 1:1–2 (ESV)*

> *"To Timothy, my beloved child: Grace, mercy, and peace from God the Father and Christ Jesus our Lord."*
>
> *2 Timothy 1:2 (ESV)*

> *"I hope in the Lord Jesus to send Timothy to you soon . . . For I have no one like him, who will be genuinely concerned for your welfare. . . . But you know Timothy's proven worth, how as a son with a father he has served with me in the gospel."*

Philippians 2:19–22 (ESV)

Paul's Words to the Corinthians

> *"For though you might have ten thousand instructors in Christ, yet you do not have many fathers; for in Christ Jesus I have begotten you through the gospel."*

1 Corinthians 4:15 (NKJV)

The background of this statement lies within the fact that many had made their way into the church at Corinth and there were contradictory, confusing teachings ripping the church apart with strife. Paul was appealing to his "children" in the Lord to receive him and his ministry at a higher level than all these others who had come into Corinth bringing their various doctrines which had led to sectarianism.

Let's look a bit further into this statement. The Greek word translated instructor is *paidagogos* or "boy leader"—a servant who took the children and dropped them off at school. Once he had taken the children to school, the instructor could relax until school was over. He was not expected to be concerned about what the child was learning or how he behaved.

Paul says that there were many of these instructor types of ministries in the church, but that only he was really a father to them. He reveals that there is a vast difference from a fathering influence and an instructor's influence in the lives of the people. A father is passionately concerned for every aspect of his children's well-being!

SMALL GROUP DISCUSSION:

What are the differences between an instructor and a father?

Father   Instructor

_____   _____

_____   _____

_____   _____

_____   _____

_____   _____

_____   _____

_____   _____

THE APOSTLE JOHN

We again find these tender, fatherly affections in another of Jesus's first followers, John, as he writes to his spiritual children in the tiny but fantastic little book, 3 John. Listen to John's fathering heart:

> "The elder to the beloved Gaius, whom I love in truth. Beloved, I pray that all may go well with you and that you may be in good health, as it goes well with your soul. For I rejoiced greatly when the brothers came and testified to your truth, as indeed you are walking in the truth. _I have no greater joy than to hear that my children are walking in the truth._"

3 John 1–4 (NASB)

In these opening words of John to Gaius and the believers, we find the Father/Son Paradigm at work in and through this aging apostle. He speaks of Gaius as the one that he loves. He prays for Gaius's health and prosperity. Then he reveals the depths of the heart of a spiritual father or mother when he says, "I have no greater joy than to hear that my children are walking in the truth!" This, at its core, is the heart of a father or a mother. A father and mother think like this, "My greatest joy, my greatest achievement, my highest success in life is children who are walking with Jesus Christ, children who are living in the truth, children who have left the ways of darkness and are walking in the light, children in the Kingdom of God!" John was so caught up in the Father/Son Paradigm that in his gospel and the three tiny epistles, he uses the word father 117 times. He had become the embodiment of this Kingdom principle and his writings ooze with it!

THE OPERATING SYSTEM OF THE KINGDOM OF GOD

I am convinced that the Father/Son Paradigm is the very operating system of the Kingdom of God. An operating system is the behind the scenes construct that governs how a computer works. It is the program behind all the programs. It is the inner mind that governs how a computer receives information, processes information, and then uses that information.

Let's take a look as we close this chapter, at the very last words of the Old Testament and the opening of the New Testament:

> "Behold, I will send you Elijah the prophet
> Before the coming of the great and dreadful
> day of the LORD. And he will turn <u>The hearts
> of the fathers</u> to the children, And <u>the hearts
> of the children</u> to their fathers, Lest I come

and strike the earth with a curse."
Malachi 4:5–6 (NKJV)

The Old Testament ends with a great promise and warning. This promise and warning set the spiritual atmosphere for the coming of the Son of God and the breaking in of His mighty reign—the Kingdom of God. So what is the Spirit saying to us through these final prophetic words closing out the record of Old Testament Scripture?

First, the phrase "the great and dreadful day of the LORD" speaks of the first and second coming of Jesus. We must remember that when Jesus came, He did not simply come as a suffering servant to win our salvation, but He also came as the King of a spiritual kingdom in the spiritual realm, and that realm of the Kingdom was breaking into the earth changing everything. Jesus Himself spoke of John the Baptist, of this promised Elijah ministry, and John's own message was that he had been sent to "prepare the way of the Lord."

So what was to happen as a precursor to His first coming ushering in the manifestation of His Kingdom and then would again occur prior to His second coming? God would send forth the "spirit" of Elijah and this spirit would bring about one work— it would restore the Father/Son Paradigm as the operating system of life. It would put an end to the professionalism of ministry in Jesus's day and ours. It would restore multigenerational, relational investment as the operating system of life. I am convinced that this is the purest atmosphere that all things Kingdom grow within. It is the very atmosphere of heaven for that is how heaven works—the Father loves the Son and gives all things into His hands and the Son honors, loves, and lives <u>from</u> the Father and <u>for</u> the Father and His will. Heaven operates on this paradigm and the Kingdom of earth does too!

Let's look at one last thing, the opening words of the New Testament. "The historical record of Jesus Christ, the Son of

David, the Son of Abraham: Abraham fathered Isaac, Isaac fathered Jacob, Jacob fathered Judah and his brothers" (Matthew 1:1–2 HCSB). Just as the Old Testament closes with the promise that God will restore fatherhood and sonship as the preparation for the coming of His Son and His Kingdom, the New Testament begins by calling Jesus the "Son of David", and David the "Son of Abraham." Then it lists 42 generations of fathers and sons! Look at the language: "Abraham fathered Isaac, Isaac fathered Jacob." It speaks of fathering and sonship 42 times at the opening of the New Testament directly after God ends the record of the Old Testament with the promise of restoring the Father/Son Paradigm before the coming of the Son of God.

God is screaming a very clear message: My Son and His Kingdom come into the world and operate most effectively through this multigenerational relational way of life. The Father/ Son Paradigm is the very operating system of the Kingdom of God and we had better get ourselves aligned with it or the Kingdom will either run us over or pass us by.

PART ONE

THE SPIRITUAL JOURNEY: FROM SLAVES AND ORPHANS TO SONS

As you begin this first section of this booklet, I would like to tell you my purpose to it: You cannot live life well as a spiritual father or mother if you do not first learn to live with the Father as a son or daughter. The Father/Son Paradigm must first work heavenward before it can operate at its true capacity earthward. The way we relate to the Father in heaven as genuine, mature sons empowers the life of attempting to live with the younger generations around us as fathers and mothers. May God bless you with the revelation of His Father heart as we delve into the Father/Son Paradigm!

CHAPTER THREE

JESUS AND HIS FATHER

So where do we begin? What's the starting point in this journey into the Father/Son Paradigm? Why really, it's quite simple. Everything in the Kingdom begins by going back to Jesus. He is and always will be our guide, our model, and the door into the new and next of the Kingdom of God. The beginning place of this journey is to see how Jesus lived with His Father and enter into that same kind of relationship.

I believe it's impossible to make the practical steps without first entering into the spiritual reality, for you see the Father/Son Paradigm works in two ways. It's first a vertical reality between each of us and the Father. And as we enter into this spiritual reality as genuine sons of the Father and experience His Fatherhood over our lives, it releases the power and the wisdom for us to operate in the horizontal/relational realm by becoming fathers and mothers to the emerging generations of Christ followers.

Jesus walked with God so differently than the other religious leaders of His day. He made extraordinary statements about His Father's love for Him, His delight in the Father, and in doing His will. He modeled this life; He demonstrated its reality; and He described its possibility in His many teachings and illustrations. He is the perfect example of the Father/Son Paradigm at work, so let's jump right in and see what we might learn from Him.

THE GOD OF JUDAISM

When Jesus burst upon the scene in Israel, He came to a people who were oppressed in many ways. Perhaps the greatest source of their oppression was their view of God. The religious leaders had developed and taught a view of God, which brought fear, bondage, and lifeless religion. Here were some aspects of what their God was like that they taught:

- *God was very distant and near impossible to approach.*

- *He was portrayed as a terrible Master that could never be pleased.*

- *One only came to Him through a complex set of rules and traditions—that no human could possibly keep!*

- *He was such a fearsome Being that most people lived under a spiritual cloud of oppression and guilt.*

- *The Jewish people never even said His name out of fear of speaking it incorrectly which would incur His wrath! As a result of this view of God, the people of God developed a wrong perception of themselves as well:*

- *They saw themselves as beggars who only would receive pennies from the Master.*

- *They saw themselves as slaves who could never please or appease the harsh Taskmaster.*

- *Above all, they were orphans alone in the world without a Father.*

SMALL GROUP DISCUSSION:

Discuss as many ways that this way of thinking about God and ourselves could possibly influence your life.

BIBLE STUDY:

Look at the following verses and describe the picture that Jesus paints of God. Is this the way most people see Him today? Is this the way YOU see Him?

Matthew 5:43–45; 6:1–9; 7:11; Luke 15:11–32; James 1:17

THE GOD OF THE KINGDOM: FATHER

When Jesus began His ministry, He painted such a different picture of God with both His daily life and His words. It was a picture that would liberate people and draw them near to the Father instead of driving them away. He clearly demonstrated this new Kingdom paradigm in both life and word, and He opened for us a new spiritual reality that is more wonderful than our wildest dreams—God as our Father and we, His Sons and Daughters!

JESUS'S LIFESTYLE WITH THE FATHER

So what WAS His life like? What was it like between He and the Father. A great beginning place is His baptism. As Jesus came up from the water and began to pray, His Father broke onto the scene and could not help but gush affection over and upon His Son! In Matthew it records, "This, is My beloved Son in whom I'm well pleased!" Luke records the incident in Jesus's life like this, "You are My beloved Son; in You I am well pleased!" Why the discrepancy? Why the difference? Because that is exactly what happened! The Father was both publicly and personally affirming His love and pleasure over His Son, Jesus, the son of Mary from the village of Nazareth.

Let's take a closer look at the words of the Father.

- *"This is (You are)":* The Father was declaring to the world and personally to Jesus Himself who HE was and who Jesus was to Him. I am His Father! He is My Son! That's who I am and that's who He is. This whole Kingdom thing is about a Father and a Son. Notice what He didn't say: This is My Christ. This is your Savior. This is the great King of the emerging Kingdom. This is your teacher and guide. This is . . . All of these things are true but in the Kingdom of God, it all begins with I am Your Father and You are My Son! The Father/Son Paradigm is one of the foundation stones that everything works from, and if we don't get this right, most everything else will somehow be off, somehow broken.

- *"Beloved":* The Father begins the public life of Jesus where His messianic ministry is launched with this word: I love Him. My affection is so, so great for My Son. He is My beloved. Jesus, You are My beloved. Do you want to know how I feel about You? I'm smitten with love! This was cataclysmic in the world of Jesus. That the fearsome God of Judaism would commit Himself to a single man in this kind of tender affection and compassionate love. Love, the love of a perfect Father for His children, is the only possible place to begin in the Kingdom of God. We can never love Him until His tender, unearned, undeserved affections overcome our fears and our feelings of unworthiness and distance. Love is the beginning of everything in the Kingdom of God—not our love but our Father's!

- *"With Him (You) I am well pleased":* Long before Jesus preached His first sermon, healed His first leper, or showed compassion to a mother who had just lost her only son, the Father stated the very foundational DNA of the relationship: I'm so, so pleased with Him (You). In the world Jesus stepped into, finding God's pleasure was a lifelong task of incredibly hard work that no one ever attained to. It was an impossible goal with the God they had been presented! But now, right beside this river where this man, Jesus Bar-Joseph, had been baptized with all the other sinners by John the Baptizer, God breaks heaven's silence with a crazy statement, Jesus, My Son, I'm so pleased with You. How could this *be? What? Right after His baptism? He hadn't done anything great yet! For all those standing there, Jesus was simply another sinful man who had come to have his guilt washed away and make himself right with God. They had no idea that He was the sinless Son of God who had been tempted in every way as they, but yet had never succumbed to the seductions of sin and the flesh. He was one of them—a sinner in need of forgiveness. It was over this man with these very things in the minds of the people that His Father spoke these words. Notice that God did not seek to clarify, Oh, and He is perfect. He is going to do miracles, and die for you all. No, He simply let them believe Jesus was one of them in the water, washing all of His filth and guilt away. This is cataclysmic when you think about it. God was saying, When you first come to me, while you are still bad, still evil in heart, just beginning this journey, I am yours and you are Mine. I am pleased with you from the very beginning. Not after you have become all cleaned up and perfect. I am pleased with you not on the basis of your condition, but on the basis of you are Mine and I am your Father. It's the Father/Son Paradigm at work. It breaks all the "God rules" that we have come to believe.*

Jesus began His messianic mission FROM the pleasure of a Father. The Father was pleased purely because He was His. This is one of the most needed revelations in the life of every child. I am convinced as Henri Nouwen says that the height of all spirituality in the Kingdom of God is hearing the God of all the universes say, "You are My beloved, My son, My daughter. Oh, I am so, so very pleased with you!" And our response is usually, "But God, have you not seen me when I . . . Don't you know that I . . . But God, surely, I must . . . No! "You are My son, My daughter. I love you and all My affections are for you. I love you. I enjoy you. You are Mine!"

A second glimpse we have into this intimate fellowship of Jesus and His Father was seen a few years earlier when Jesus was lecturing at the temple at 12 years old. When His parents finally found Him after searching for just under a week and they began to scold Him, He seems in no way upset and even mystified that they didn't know where He would be. His response, "Didn't you know that I must be about (or in) the things of My Father." For Jesus, the things of His Father were His things. He was intimately and inextricably linked to the Father's will, the Father's desires, the Father's business. It was never a "ministry" to Him—it was His Father's business—the family business!

Listen to a few of His own words about He and the Father:

- *"My Father is working until now, and I am working"* (John 5:17 ESV).

- *"Truly, truly, I say to you, the Son can do nothing of his own accord, but only what he sees the Father doing. For whatever the Father does, that the Son does likewise. For the Father loves the Son and shows him all that he himself is doing"* (John 5:19–20 ESV).

- *"I have come in my Father's name"* (John 5:43 ESV).

- *"If you knew me, you would know my Father also"* (John 8:19 ESV).

Jesus's Description of the Father

If we were to examine all or even most of the Father describing statements Jesus made about God, this volume would go far beyond its desired length, but let's take a peek at a few of His declarations. Jesus said:

- *"When you pray, say, 'Our Father.'"* *This seems so basic or elementary to us, but for the Israelite of Jesus's day, this was monumental.* *"Father? I can call Him Father? Is that possible? Legal? Available?"* *We have no idea how this one little statement by Jesus, the first Son in this new Kingdom paradigm, challenged the status quo of His day.*

- *"If you then, who are evil, know how to give good gifts to your children, how much more will your Father who is in heaven give good things to those who ask him!"* (Matthew 7:11 HCSB) *For me, this one statement says it all, "How much more your Father in heaven." That is the essence of His description of the Father, how much more our Father!*

- *"Fear not, little flock, for it is your Father's good pleasure to give you the kingdom" (Luke 12:32 ESV). This declaration gets at the very heart of God. It gives Him pleasure, great pleasure to lavish upon us His greatest treasure—the Kingdom of God.*

We could go on and on, but I think you get the point. As Jesus erupted onto the Jewish scene and began to talk about God as His Father and ours, He utterly redefined heaven's Master and Creator. He is a Father. Not just a Father, but our Father, and at His very core is ultimate goodness and love. Jesus's mission included fully redefining the Father for the world, "No one has ever seen God; the only God, who is at the Father's side, <u>he has made him known</u>" (John 1:18 ESV).

JESUS'S INVITATION FOR US TO KNOW AND LIVE WITH THE FATHER

As His ministry went on, it became apparent to all who followed Him or were at least with Him for longer periods that the very life He lived was not singular, but rather a picture, an example of what He had come to instill as the basic Kingdom pattern of life on earth for all who would enter. It's called the Father/Son Paradigm! It is the fundamental way to relate to heaven—He's our Father, we are His children, and in us is all of His delight! What Jesus was and experienced as the only begotten of the Father, we now share in as adopted children. What He had from eternity past and experienced as a man upon the earth, we enter into by grace.

> *"If we preach the Kingdom without the Fatherhood of God, the Kingdom can seem very severe and harsh."*
>
> *Alan Vincent*

But when we see the Kingdom in terms of a beloved Son lovingly obeying His Father, it makes it a much more wonderful relationship. Jesus did not find it hard to live in the Kingdom; it was His absolute joy. It was joy because of the love relationship between the Father and the Son. And so it is with those who truly enter the Kingdom of God.

GENUINE SONSHIP: THE EXPRESSION OF A KINGDOM HEART

One of the truest tests of a person discovering, entering, and experiencing the Kingdom is sonship—are they living as sons or slaves. Many may have heard and even quoted verses about being sons of God, but when we look at their lives, their faith, and their hearts, we see nothing but beggars/slaves. The goal of the religious spirit is to always drag us back into a slave's thinking and life.

John lived longer with the Lord and perhaps experienced more of the Kingdom than any man. All of his writings took place from around AD 90–100 after he had walked with God for 60–70 years. What can we learn from His writings? He knew the Father. In 1 John 3:1, it is as if his spirit is exploding with this truth when he writes, *"Behold what manner of love the Father has given to us, that we should be called the children of God. And that is what we are!"* (BSB)

SMALL GROUP DISCUSSION:

What are 10 things that we can transfer to our lives from Jesus's relationship with His Father?

SONS OR SLAVES

My journey into the Kingdom with Jesus is marked with a myriad of ups and downs, ins and outs, wins and losses. One of the colossal breakthroughs in my walk with Jesus in this Kingdom reality was the answering of this elemental question: Who am I with God? In the opening days of my Christian journey, it was sheer bliss. Jesus was the center, the Bible was sweet, and life was grand, but as my desire to know Him more and be of use to Him increased, I began to feel like I never measured up. I began to feel that there was always something more I should be doing and that my sinful nature was just, well, "too sinful." About five years into my Christian journey, I felt far more like a slave that could never do enough to please the Master than a son who was a delight to His heavenly Father. Later, I discovered that this was common in the New Testament Church days as well. Whew! What a relief.

When Paul planted the church in Galatia, he instilled within it a pure gospel—the gospel of the Kingdom of God, inaugurated by Jesus Christ, founded upon the grace of God. After some time, Jewish teachers known as Judaizers, who claimed to follow Jesus, snuck into the church and began to instill another gospel, the gospel of Jesus plus keeping the Law. It went something like this, "If you really want to enter the Kingdom of God and know God, then you must receive Jesus and keep the Law. There is no way to know God or relate to Him unless you follow the Law. Jesus is God's Son, but He was also a Jew and He kept the Law. If Jesus related to God through keeping the Law, so must you!"

The results were disastrous! The Galatian believers began to leave the pure life of faith in Jesus and began to build their lives upon dead works. The end result was that they left living as sons of God and began to live as slaves again. Listen to the words of Paul:

- *"O foolish Galatians! Who has bewitched you? It was before your eyes that Jesus Christ was publicly* portrayed as crucified. Let me ask you only this: Did you receive the Spirit by works of the law or by hearing with faith? Are you so foolish? Having begun by the Spirit, are you now being perfected by the flesh?" (Galatians 3:1–3 ESV)

- "So then, those who are of faith are blessed along with Abraham, the man of faith. For all who rely on works of the law are under a curse" (Galatians 3:9–10 ESV).

- "But when the fullness of time had come, God sent forth his Son, born of woman, born under the law, to redeem those who were under the law, so that we might receive adoption as sons. And because you are sons, God has sent the Spirit of his Son into our hearts, crying, 'Abba! Father!'" (Galatians 4:4–6 ESV)

- Paul's grand conclusion of these things: "So you are no longer a slave, but a son, and if a son, then an heir through God!" (Galatians 4:7 ESV)

To Paul, living in this Kingdom with the pure gospel of Jesus Christ had only one reasonable result—you are no longer a slave. You are a son! The Father/Son Paradigm is at the center of Paul's theology, and for him, one of the great battles with the spirits of darkness in this Kingdom war was over our sonship and God's Fatherhood.

ARE YOU LIVING AS A SLAVE OR A SON?

Over the years, I've discovered this is a trap of the enemy for most sincere hearted followers of Jesus. I discovered there are some common traits of slaves and sons I want to share with you for you to examine your own Kingdom walk:

1. A servant does not live in the Father's house because his relationship to the Master is command oriented. The son lives with the Father because his relationship is based on family.

Jesus answered them, "Most assuredly, I say to you, whoever commits sin is a slave of sin. And a *slave does not abide in the house forever, but a son abides forever."*

John 8:34–35 (NKJV)

- *A servant or slave is hired or purchased to serve—to perform duties given to him by the master. When he correctly does his work, he pleases the master and is rewarded. However, should he fail to do a good job, punishment would be meted out. But the final result is that he is never welcomed to live in the father's house, enjoy the father's blessings, eat at the father's table, or have sweet access to the father. He belongs in the slave or servant quarters somewhere out back!*

- *This is the relationship that many are bound in—believing that acceptance and approval by God are based on what they do—their performance. These sincere believers are frustrated because they will never be "good enough" to earn the Father's love. The end result is that they live lives away from the intimate presence of the Father because they don't belong in "His house"; they belong in the servants' quarters outside.*

- *A son's relationship to the father, on the other hand, is based on familial love, not performance. The son does his father's will because of their relationship, not out of a sense of performance based duty. He is a faithful servant of his father who will always do his best out of love for his father and his father's love for him. There will be times when the father will become disappointed with the son because of bad behavior, but he remains the father and the son remains the son, despite the son's poor behavior or performance. Once a son, always a son! The end result of this kind of life is living in the Father's house. We have access and intimacy with the Father because we are His and that gives us absolute access to His presence!*

- *When Queen Elizabeth of England ascended the monarchy in 1953, her husband, Prince Phillip, held a very important position within the realm. He was the distributor of kingdom funds for benevolence and the care of the poor. Servants of the kingdom would gain a 15-minute audience with the Prince in which they* would state their case and sell their idea on how to use the kingdom's resources for good.

- A Christian man obtained one of these brief interviews, rehearsed his sales pitch a 100 times and then entered the private office of the Prince one day. About three minutes into his presentation, a side door of the office flung open and one of the Monarch's young sons burst into the room. "Papa, my toy. It's broken. Will you fix it?" Prince Phillip turned to the man and said, "Excuse me. I must attend to my son." After a painstaking few minutes with the boy's toy, he said, "Now run along to your play and let me finish talking with this gentleman." The Prince looked at his watch and said, "Sir, you have three more minutes." The man failed to obtain his financial grant, but learned the greatest lesson of his life: "Servants have very limited access to the King, but sons have a special, intimate door into the King's office because they are a son. They live IN the house!"

What about you? Are you more like a slave or a son?

2. The slave only hears enough to carry out his duty, but the son receives intimate knowledge from the Father.

Many Christians are stuck in this slave-based communication trap, only finding out what God wants them to do. They don't expect God to reveal any of the "deep things" He thinks and feels. They don't feel worthy. They are always waiting for someone else to get the word of the Lord for them.

Listen to the words of Jesus as He began to unveil the glories of our communication with God as sons:

- About His own life of hearing the Father speak: "Very truly I tell you, the Son can do nothing by himself; he can do only what he sees his Father doing, because whatever the Father does the Son also does. For the Father loves the Son and shows him all he does" (John 5:19–20 NIV).

- "But the Advocate, the Holy Spirit, whom the Father will send in my name, will teach you all things and will *remind you of everything I have said to you" (John 14:26 NIV).*

- *"I have much more to say to you, more than you can now bear. But when he, the Spirit of truth, comes, he will guide you into all the truth. He will not speak on his own; he will speak only what he hears, and he will tell you what is yet to come. He will glorify me because it is from me that he will receive what he will make known to you. All that belongs to the Father is mine. That is why I said the Spirit will receive from me what he will make known to you" (John 16:12–15 NIV).*

Jesus fully expected that the sons of God would have a deep, intimate, ever developing life of communication with He and the Father by the Spirit. It is our birthright as sons! It is normal in the Kingdom of God! It is the very source of life— "Man shall not live on bread alone, but on every word that comes from the mouth of God" (Matthew 4:4 NIV).

3. The servant's relationship with his Master is governed by fear, while the son lives in the Father's love.

Fear is the foundational motivation for most slaves and servants in regard to their master.

- *Fear of not measuring up to the master's expectations.*

- *Fear of not receiving the reward for his service.*

- *Fear of punishment should he fail to do the master's will.*

- *Fear that, should he not fully please the master, his services could be terminated.*

- *Fear, fear, fear.*

- *Through the spirit of bondage, Satan himself wants to keep us from recognizing and living in our inheritance as sons of God He wants to keep us from that which Jesus purchased on the Cross. Satan wants to deceive us and distort the truth; he wants us to believe that we must work to be accepted, but that we can never be good enough to please God. This is the whole plan of religion. It is bondage and only leads to failure and fear. Paul wrote, "The Spirit you received does not make you slaves, so that you live in fear again; rather, the Spirit you received brought about your adoption to sonship. And by him we cry, 'Abba, Father.' The Spirit himself testifies with our spirit that we are God's children" (Romans 8:15–16 NIV).*

- *Praise the Lord that as sons we have nothing to fear from our Master because of His perfect love for us! In fact, our Master is a Father, our Father, who loves us, desires us, and is overjoyed that we are His. Listen to the words of the apostle of love, John, "There is no fear in love; but perfect love casts out fear, because fear involves torment. But he who fears has not been made perfect in love" (1 John 4:18 NKJV).*

- *Since Jesus paid for our sins, we have nothing to fear. As sons of God, we live in His love, and fear has no place in our hearts. Jesus paid our penalty and we are now His children. He may discipline us at times, but always in love, not anger or hatred. When we fall again prey to fear, we must come again to the understanding of our position in Jesus Christ. As His children, we become so secure in our Father's love that we can rest on His promises of protection, provision, and His abiding presence.*

4. A servant works to hopefully obtain some kind of reward, but the son enjoys the entire wealth of the Father's house!

"Therefore you are no longer a slave but a son, and if a son, then an heir of God through Christ."

Galatians 4:7 (NKJV)

"heirs of God and joint heirs with Christ"

Romans 8:17 (NKJV)

- *Slaves and servants work to get paid or to receive some kind of reward from their master; however, the reward is never sure and never grand! Satan wants us to stay ignorant of our glorious inheritance in Jesus Christ. He wants us to continue to see ourselves as beggars, slaves, and servants. If he can, we will live with mere "peanuts" in our pockets and live bankrupt lives of constant spiritual lack, never accessing all that is ours with the Father in Jesus Christ.*

- *When we as Christians begin to discover our place before Him as sons, and because we are sons, we are heirs, we will start to take dominion again and take back from the enemy all he has stolen from us. But, many Christians have never realized the full benefits of their inheritance. What is keeping them from it? They have never experienced the joy of belonging in the Father's house.*

- *Jesus, the Son of man, has inherited all things through His victory on the Cross. Now we as God's children and because of the New Covenant become joint heirs with Him. We receive this inheritance, not because of anything we might do, but because of who He is and our relationship to Him. Our inheritance is a gift from the Father, and now it's time to enter into the house and claim it!*

- *My friends! It's time to throw off the spirit of slavery and take our place as the sons of God. It's time to say, "No more! That's not true. That's not who I am. I am a son of God with the full rights and resources of a son!" Oh how wonderful to receive and believe these words, "You are My beloved Son, in whom I am well pleased" (Mark 1:11 NKJV).*

CHAPTER FOUR

THE ORPHAN SPIRIT

Years ago, a young man stood in a courtroom to be sentenced for forgery. The judge had known the boy since his childhood, for the boy's father had been a famous legal writer, with his work on The Law of Trusts being the most exhaustive work on the subject in existence. "Do you remember your father," asked the judge sternly, "that father whom you have disgraced?" The young prisoner answered, "I remember him perfectly. When I went to him for advice or companionship, he would look up from his book on The Law of Trusts, and say, 'Run away, boy, I am busy.' My father finished his book, and here I am."

The great lawyer had been a success in his work but had failed as a father. His son was burdened with a curse—the curse of growing into manhood with no father's love, guidance, or touch. He grew up with a man who had helped bring him into the world, but without a father to love and guide him in that journey through the world. The boy was an orphan!

I wonder how many of us have grown up in similar ways? I wonder how many hearts THE Father has turned to Himself have grown up without the great gift of being fathered by someone who looks like Him and acts like Him? I wonder how many of us have grown up with the spirit of an orphan? I am convinced that one of the greatest crises that we face upon the earth today is fatherlessness leading to an orphan spirit.

When I use the word "spirit" in this context, I am not referring to some grand demonic power, but rather an attitude, a way of looking at life, a way of processing all things that come your way. The Bible uses one of the words for spirit in this way also. It can mean a spiritual entity or an attitude of heart and mind. I also want to acknowledge that this phrase, "orphan spirit," is not used in the New Testament at all, but has been developed over time to describe this phenomenon amongst us that we all can testify as truth—people who grow up without a fathering/mothering presence share similar traits that are unhealthy at best and destructive at worst. Open your heart as you read further about the orphan spirit.

THE NEED FOR NATURAL FATHERS

To say that there is a crisis in our nation, the United States of America, and ever growing in the world around us is probably not an overstatement. In every measurable area of life, children who grow up without a truly present, engaged father suffer greater risk of the formation of an unhealthy life that leads to all sorts of damage and problems. It is estimated that in our nation alone, almost 25 million children are growing up without a present father. Listen to what some of the experts in their field say about the absence of fathers in children's lives:

- *"Fatherlessness is having a great impact on education. . . . Children are four times more likely to be poor if the father is not around. And we know that poverty is heavily associated with academic success . . . Dropping out of school, growing up fatherless, and incarceration appear to be connected. One study . . . shows that seven out of ten high school dropouts are fatherless[2]."*

- *"The research . . . says that girls are twice as likely to suffer from obesity without the father present. They're four times more likely to get pregnant as teenagers[3]."*

- *"We're hearing a lot about teen suicide these days. [Data] . . . suggest that children growing up without a father are more than twice as likely to commit suicide[4]."*

- *President Barack Obama, who was raised in a single-mother household stated in his 2008 Father's Day speech: "Of all the rocks upon which we build our lives, we are reminded today that family is most important. And we are called to recognize and honor how critical every father is to that foundation. They are teachers and coaches. They are mentors and role models. They are examples of success and the men who constantly push us toward it. But if we are honest with ourselves, we'll admit that too many fathers are missing—missing from too many lives and too many homes. They have abandoned their responsibilities, acting like boys instead of men. And the foundations of our families are weaker because of it."*

SPIRITUAL FATHERS

What about children of God growing up without fathering and mothering figures in their spiritual lives? One leader and church father stated, "The Church of Jesus looks more like a great orphanage than a spiritual family!" Many of us ministers in the world have become proficient in everything except fathering and mothering. We are great preachers, excellent teachers, and world class organizers who plan to the last detail. But are we those who step out from behind the pulpit, opening our homes and lives to the younger generation who need connection and help from those who've gone before them? Have we become the mothering and fathering generation raising up mature and healthy sons and daughters? This lack of spiritual fathers has surely contributed to the epidemic of the orphan spirit across the church. Where there is no presence of true parenting in the daily life of the children of God, the void causes an orphan's heart and mind.

Our spiritual father is Jack Taylor, an 86-year-old master of fathering. I've never seen a man who knows the Father as he does, so intimately, affectionately, and freely and then lives from that reality with the next generation of young men and women as a spiritual papa. We all affectionately call him Papa Jack because that is truly who he is. Jack says often, "We all need an orphanectomy so we can live whole and fruitful lives!"

The Promise and the Curse

Let's go to the Scriptures and see how this plays out in the narrative of the Bible. The last statement of the Old Testament speaks of a mighty promise that God will carry out, but the very last words also speak of a curse:

> *"Behold, I am going to send you Elijah the prophet before the coming of the great and terrible day of the LORD. He will restore the hearts of the fathers to their children and the hearts of the children to their fathers, so that I will not come and smite the land with a curse."*
>
> *Malachi 4:5–6 (NASB)*

THE PROMISE

The promise spoken of here is that God will send the spirit of His servant Elijah (a man who was a great father to Elisha), and this Spirit will restore fathering and sonship in the last days. As I shared earlier, Elijah was able to impart so much to Elisha that when Elisha took over, He began his ministry with a double portion of anointing, and was able to completely finish the task that Elijah did not. Elijah seemed like he never finished his task and was perhaps even a failure, but he had raised up a son that started where he left off, and the work was finished through the next generation. This is what God is promising! Father/son and mother/daughter relationships that get the job of making disciples done—where our spiritual children go further than we do and complete the great tasks that God has given us!

THE CURSE

> *"lest I come and strike the earth with a curse!"*
>
> *Malachi 4:6 (NKJV)*

THE ORPHAN SPIRIT

The only logical conclusion of what this curse might be is the orphan spirit. Where there are no fathers and sons working together, building together, is orphan living. The orphan spirit is an atmosphere and an attitude of the heart that prevents people, churches, and even cities from becoming all they can be in God. It is characterized by having grown up without ever having true discipleship or parental input or impartation. Often, the motto of the people and groups are, "I grew up on my own."

Satan has attacked fatherhood, both in the natural realm and the spiritual, in order to rob us of spiritual parents and create an orphan spirit in the church. Many churches have operated more like orphanages than spiritual families, creating programs to raise people rather than relationships. Most of the believers who have never been properly discipled (those who cannot point to a person or group of people who served as spiritual parents for them) possess an orphan spirit to some degree. This spirit is hampering the Body of Christ greatly these days. Only fathers rising up and taking their places can break the curse of the orphan spirit of the church.

Author Jim Mattera says, "Ever since Adam and Eve were alienated from God the Father in the Garden of Eden, an orphan spirit has permeated the earth, causing untold damage! (By 'orphan,' I am referring to a sense of abandonment, loneliness, alienation, and isolation.) Almost immediately after the Fall in Eden, the fruit of this orphan spirit resulted in jealousy, culminating in Cain murdering his brother Abel because God the Father didn't receive Cain's offering."

MARKS OF THE ORPHAN SPIRIT

See God as Their Master: Their relationship with God is not based upon the Father's great love and mercy. Instead, He is their Master. There is usually an unhealthy fear of God and very little true trust or faith. They are constantly working to earn His love and approval, where a mature son lives from the place of acceptance and being loved.

Independent and Self-Reliant: People with an orphan spirit feel they have "to make it on their own," and will continue to do so. The deep interconnection of loving relationships and a true sense of need for others is not displayed. It may seem to exist outwardly, but when things get tough, the "I will make it on my own" attitude comes out. On the other hand, true sons of the Father live deep lives of interconnected relationships, both giving and receiving. They know their heavenly Father is at work and often through His children all around.

Insecurity: Most people with an orphan spirit are very insecure. It shows in them whether they are leaders or followers. Their self-worth is fragile and is easily damaged. This can be expressed through people being very loud and aggressive or quiet and shy. There is often an innate fear of failure even while striving desperately to succeed. Sons, mature sons, have an ever growing sense of security that emanates from their Father's love, approval, and a place at the table with His other children.

Fight and Grab for What They Want: People who grow up with an orphan spirit learn to grab for what they want. They become skilled manipulators, often twisting the truth to get their needs met. They are often grabbers and manipulators, just like Jacob was in the Bible. Because God is a Master that can't be expected to have their best interest in His mind, they take it upon themselves to get what they need or want. Sons on the other hand, have an innate trust of the Father and know He is ultimately in charge of what comes their way. They trust the Father and believe Him for their supply of all things in life's journey.

Do Not Trust Authorities Over Them: Another mark of the orphan heart is a lack of trust of spiritual authorities or even governmental authorities. The orphan believes that these people don't exist to prosper people; instead, they believe that leaders exist only to get things out of people and to tell others what to do. The orphan spirit prevents people from seeing their authorities as wonderful ministers of God placed over them for their good. Sons on the other hand, relate well and submit when and where needed. Their inner security creates an attitude of trust and a belief in the good motives of others around them.

Relationships With Peers Often Marked by Competition or Jealousy: Because those with an orphan mindset did not grow up in a proper family environment (whether in the natural or spiritual), their relationships with others are often marked by negative feelings and negative attitudes, rather than love, humility, and unity. If they feel they have to grab and reach for every good thing, they can't handle the success and blessing of others. They often show this by criticism and judgmentalism. Sons are able to rejoice in the good of others around them because they know that there is plenty of room at the Father's table and plenty of goodness and riches in the Father's house. They realize that this thing really is a family and when another in the Body of Christ succeeds, it's their success too.

Orphans Often "Medicate" Themselves: People with an orphan spirit will live a life of medicating their internal emptiness with things from this world both good and bad. Worse case scenario, you see a constant reversion to different forms of addictions, and best case scenario, these orphan hearted believers medicate with the good things of this world—appearance, accumulation, and self-indulgence. But mature sons are able to balance all of these things in their proper place remaining free from being controlled by any of them. The acceptance of the Father and His joy fill them with internal fulfillment that doesn't leave that empty void which must be filled.

Often Very Talented, but Plagued With Character Issues: Often, people with the orphan spirit show great talent, but are plagued with all kinds of character issues. Many of the basic traits for successful relationships, organization, decision making, and other areas of character never developed. Very often, their lives are self-serving behind the scenes and eventually self-destructing along the way. Sons know their character is under constant correction and transformation by the Father; they even open their hearts to brothers and sisters who desire to be a part of the transformation process. Orphans MUST protect their hearts at all cost, so when those around them speak into their character, they often rise up in blatant self-defense or withdraw all together.

The Orphan Spirit Uses People as Objects to Fulfill Their Goals: Those with an orphan spirit tend to use people as objects to accomplish their goals. They objectify people manipulating them with words, threatening them, or anything else necessary to control them to get what they desire. Mature sons always serve others, putting their good first for the sake of the Kingdom of God. They never treat others as objects to be used, but as people to be loved and served.

Stunted Growth (Never Mature Fully): The foremost trait in those of us with an orphan mentality is an immaturity that is never overcome. They never mature in their character, their calling or faith. They are stunted in growth, and unless something happens they just don't have the inner capacity to mature. Funny thing is, we were never meant to have the capacity to mature on our own. Sons rely both on their heavenly Father and those He places in their lives for the maturity process. They realize, "It takes a village to raise a child, and I am that child!"

It seems that we have churches full of these types of people—fragile, weak, undeveloped, insecure, and purposeless people, and the problem is that many of the orphan-hearted in our world have arisen into leadership.

Many years ago as I began to travel the globe, I met a tremendously talented young man. You know, the kind of guy that makes you a bit envious and jealous. It seemed that there was nothing he couldn't do. He was a tremendous preacher, a gifted intellect, an able and often captivating leader, a musician who could play any instrument he picked up, and a gifted craftsman with his hands. There was nothing this guy could not do. Over the years, I watched him serve in the church until he eventually became a senior pastor of a small church in a small village in his nation. No one really expected very much from this tiny beginning in this village in the middle of nowhere, but the church began to grow. And it grew, and it grew, and it grew. It became a model church for many churches in the larger villages and cities around it. Leaders began to arise. It was a marvel to see until . . . until it all blew up. You see the young man had grown up never knowing his father and had a mother that worked several jobs just to feed the family. He grew up on his own. He had an orphan spirit. The whole thing blew apart as his character issues glaringly came to the surface. He became controlling with anyone who questioned his authority. His sexuality broke down as did his family. Everything was lost from this beautiful beginning. This is the power of an unhealed orphan heart.

BREAKING THE CURSE

In Malachi 4, God gives the solution to the curse of an orphan-hearted generation: fathers and mothers. God says that in these last days, His Spirit will move to bring about a great revival in the area of spiritual fathering and mothering. This and this alone will break the curse and bring God's blessing back upon the land. At the end of Jesus's life, in the context of the coming of the Holy Spirit, Jesus Himself makes a very interesting statement, "I will not leave you as orphans; I will come to you" (John 14:18 ESV). Why would He say that if they had never felt like spiritual orphans before? Why would He have said these words if the possibility of feeling like and living as an orphan was not possible in these original disciples after He left? He seems to be saying that one of the mighty works of this Spirit of Truth, the Holy Spirit, was to destroy the orphan spirit and enable us to live lives as true, mature sons of God and operate as a healthy family with one another.

APPLICATION:

Read back through the list of characteristics of one with an orphan spirit and ask yourself: Which of these traits appear in your life? Do you see them in the lives of others around you? What is the answer to this curse upon our land?

Spend the next 10 minutes in prayer. Ask God to keep His promises in your own life, your church, and your nation. Ask God for personal healing and maturity. Ask Him to send His Spirit to keep this promise of Jesus that we would not be left as orphans. Ask Him for healthy fathers and mothers to rise up in the church and in the world, doing their parts. He will hear and grant your requests, if you will only ask.

CHAPTER FIVE

LEGALISM: THE ENEMY OF SONSHIP

I'll never forget my early beginnings in the Kingdom of God. Saved as a 15-year-old boy reading a story about Jesus in my bedroom only to awaken the next morning to a completely different kind of person, my world was turned on its head by this Man, Christ Jesus. I met the Spirit at 20 in an auditorium at Texas Tech University while listening to a man share on giving and generosity. Funny isn't it? Those early years were filled with so much joy and peace in Jesus. It was like heaven came down and glory filled my heart until while at the university I mentioned above, I became involved with a radical campus ministry that preached a message of extreme holiness and ultra legalism. They were so zealous and had helped introduce me to the Holy Spirit. It seemed so right, but it was so, so wrong.

The message went something like this: do more, fast more, pray more, and quit sinning. If you want God to be happy with you, you have to do more. God is angry with you when you sin and if you sin too much, you've lost your salvation and must be saved all over again. They had a rule for most everything. They even told you who you could spend time with of the opposite sex and wanted to see your bank account regularly to make sure you weren't misusing money or being materialistic. I bought the whole thing—hook, line and sinker, and in the midst of it I left my first love and entered the world of becoming an orphan and slave through the pathway of legalism.

You see, legalism is an enemy of the journey into sonship. The two are polar opposites and cannot exist in the same room or the same heart. It takes the message of grace revealing God as Father to nurture the heart into being a son, where the anti-gospel of legalism always natures the heart of orphan slaves.

THE MESSAGE YOU BELIEVE DEFINES THE GOD THAT YOU FOLLOW

The message you believe and live under in the Kingdom of God defines who God is to you and therefore the "rules" of how you must relate to Him. A legalistic message—a belief system built upon keeping rules of doing the right thing, not doing the wrong thing, and always doing more. This always lowers the view of God from being a Father to an unbending Judge, and a harsh and holy Master who cannot be pleased, no matter how much you do!

Paul ran into this heresy of legalism everywhere he took the gospel, either from the Jews who were already there or from a group of Jewish believers in Jesus who taught that trusting in Jesus alone was not enough, you also had to keep the Law of Moses. Listen to some of the things Paul says:

- *"For Christ is the end of the law for righteousness to everyone who believes" (Romans 10:4 ESV).*

- *"Now before faith came, we were held captive under the law, imprisoned until the coming faith" (Galatians 3:23 ESV).*

- *"But now that faith has come, we are no longer under a guardian [the Law], for in Christ Jesus you are all sons of God, through faith" (Galatians 3:25–26 ESV).*

We could go on and on through Jesus's words and Paul's teaching giving us insight into this battle with a legalistic body of "truth." The bottom line is that it makes God out as a harsh Judge and a terrible Master that no one can please or freely approach with confidence, and no one can really ever be close to Him. Is this the God that you serve?

The result of living under this heresy is that you are always caught in the performance trap ending up a beggar, a slave, and an orphan in your heart. It's like you live your life on a treadmill and He is always watching, expecting you to make progress in faith, holiness, and service, but the higher you turn up the speed, you still get nowhere. Then you look around you and see others progressing, but you're there on that treadmill of legalism running, always running but going nowhere, so what do you do? Turn it up a little more—if I can just do more, more, more, more! Eventually you can't do more and you give up trying. You might not walk away from Jesus, but you simply allow your burning heart to grow cold and dry and stop going after more of Jesus because the more you do, it leads to nowhere. The Performance Trap!

REFLECTION:

The spirit behind the legalistic message creates a way of thinking about relating to God. It creates the idea that all life with God begins with this—I MUST . . . If your first and deepest thought of relating to God is I MUST . . . , you are caught in the performance trap of legalism and will struggle ever moving into the life of sonship you were destined for. Describe your deepest core thought of relating to God. Does it begin with I MUST?

GRACE, AND GRACE ALONE REVEALS THE FATHER

When Jesus stepped onto the scene, His message had its very roots in the grace of a good Father and not the legalism of His day. John the Beloved said, "For from his fullness we have all received, grace upon grace. For the law was given through

Moses; <u>grace and truth</u> came through Jesus Christ" (John 1:16–17 ESV). Jesus brought forth the reality of God's great grace available for all men and it changed everything. It brought an entirely new foundation of seeing God and relating to God. No longer would we approach Him and try to relate to Him with the heart attitude of I MUST, but we would now approach Him and walk with Him through the spirit of grace which creates a mindset of He is a good Father and in Jesus it is finished therefore I can . . . !

Grace flows from the good heart of the Father and is made utterly available through Jesus's death on the Cross. It is an entirely new atmosphere to live under and to approach God through grace. Those who've discovered the grace of Jesus Christ have only one way to relate to God—FATHER.

I do not want to turn this booklet on the Father/Son Paradigm into a treatise on the message of grace, for there are many wonderful volumes written upon the subject, but I felt I had to bring this to your attention. The legalistic message always produces the I MUST attitude and reduces you to a slave and orphan. The message of God's grace, the true gospel, always begins with He is a good Father and it is finished therefore I can . . . The end result—SONS.

SMALL GROUP DISCUSSION:

Which message have you been living under? How has it affected you? How do you see legalism affecting others trying to embrace and grow into their sonship before the Father? How can you renew your mind on God's grace leading to a life of sonship?

CHAPTER SIX

THE JOURNEY HOME

Over these many years of walking with Jesus and seeking to help others discover Him and His Kingdom, I've come to a conclusion, the Father/Son Paradigm is the operating system of the Kingdom of God. It's not complicated—it's just not easy. Most of the things that are of highest priority and value in His Kingdom are not complicated, but they are very often counterintuitive to the way we've learned to live. There seems to be something always at work within us trying to work against the flow of Kingdom living. One of these inner forces that flows against the tide of Kingdom living lies in this area of truly living as sons on the deepest level. In fact, after working with 100s, no 1000s of followers of Jesus worldwide, and then observing my own inner journey, I've discovered that experiencing sonship with the Father is not an event, but rather a journey. It begins at salvation and then the new birth, but takes time and some real work to become the dominant reality of our lives.

John makes an interesting statement when he says, "But to all who did receive him, who believed in his name, he gave the right to become children of God" (John 1:12 ESV). Although Scripture is abundantly clear that we've been both born again into His family and adopted as His sons, John chooses to say that we must become children of God. The word "become" speaks of a process, a journey into the reality of the matter!

On God's side and from His point of view, it is finished, a done deal, a settled reality. We are His children, His sons, and nothing can ever challenge that in His heart or mind. He treats us as full sons with the full rights, privileges, and resources as sons right now. There's nothing we must grow in as far as He is concerned. Therein lies the problem, most often we don't live from God's point of view, we live from ours! I think that's what John was pointing to: we ARE His children on God's side of the grand equation, but in our own hearts and minds we must become a son of God. The journey is simply coming home to see ourselves and accept the heavenly identity He's bestowed upon us as sons.

John went on to say, "See what great love the Father has lavished on us, that we should be called children of God! And that is what we are! The reason the world does not know us is that it did not know him" (1 John 3:1 NIV). It seems to me that as John was writing this short epistle, he began to revel in the love of God as he wrote these words. Oh, God has shown us so much love—He allows us <u>to be called His children</u>! You know what, <u>that really is what we are</u>! This is the challenge—the challenge is finding the journey home.

THE JOURNEY

The journey begins with repentance and acknowledgement. Repentance is the act of changing our thinking. It is saying NO to lies and YES to His truth. Acknowledgement means that I bring my mind into agreement with the Word of God. "I am a son! I am His beloved! He is well pleased with me! That is who I am!" When we choose to begin the process of acknowledgement, we begin to renew our mind. The renewing of the mind is not simply putting in more good information, it is changing the source of where all information flows. Do my thoughts begin with God's reality and flow into mine or do my thoughts begin with my own feelings and experiences? It is creating entirely new starting places in our hearts and minds for our beliefs.

The second stage of the journey is learning to cooperate with the Spirit as He seeks to create a revolution within us through the Father's truth. To acknowledge the truth of our sonship and His Fatherhood without deep and consistent interaction with the Spirit is to simply play mind games with ourselves that lead nowhere. We need the Spirit to carry out His job in this journey. Listen to some of the writings of Paul on the Spirit's role in this journey home:

- *"But when the fullness of the time came, God sent forth His Son, born of a woman, born under the Law, so that He might redeem those who were under the Law, that we might receive the adoption as sons. Because you are sons, God has sent forth the Spirit of His Son into our hearts, crying, 'Abba! Father!' Therefore, you are no longer a slave, but a son; and if a son, then an heir through God"* (Galatians 4:4–7 NIV).

- *"For you did not receive the spirit of slavery to fall back into fear, but you have received the Spirit of adoption as sons, by whom we cry, 'Abba! Father!' The Spirit himself bears witness with our spirit that we are children of God"* (Romans 8:15–16 ESV).

Paul made it abundantly clear that the journey into genuine, heartfelt and mind-transformed sonship was not just the acknowledgement of truth, but the truth had to be coupled with a deep, inner working of the Spirit of sonship in our hearts. The two works of the Spirit Paul describes are first a new cry arising within us—ABBA! This is the word in Paul's world for an intimate life with a father. It would have been the word used by a little boy or girl for their daddy. It's a term of deep intimacy and true sonship. The Spirit is to work deeply within changing the natural cry of our hearts from Master, Judge, or Fearsome God to Abba. These other cries are real, and necessary at times, but the core cry of our inner man is to be first and foremost ABBA!

The second working of the Spirit coincides with this new heart cry. It is to testify with our own human spirit that we are His children. The human spirit is the nucleus of our being and the

Spirit of Jesus and the Spirit of our Father is to write a new testimony there, "You are not a slave, you are not a beggar, you are not an orphan. You are My beloved, My son in whom I am well pleased." When this new inner testimony begins to work up from our spirit into our hearts and then into our minds, we have made the sonship journey. We've come home—to Father.

To be brutally honest, this has been a long journey home for me. I began on the path of sonship, but then took a long detour down the legalism path. It was a terrible detour. As legalism did its job, I was launched into years of beggar-slave living. It was gruesome! God sent a wonderful teacher named John into our lives and he began to unfold the heart of God to us as a Father and our rightful place as sons. Perhaps 20 years ago, I began to acknowledge this truth and it has taken the Holy Spirit many years to lead me into the reality of this relationship. Even today, there are times when I find myself reverting back into feeling like an orphan (I'm out here on my own) or a slave (I'm just not doing enough; I'm sinning too much!). Be patient, it's a long but wonderful journey home.

A PARABLE ABOUT THE JOURNEY HOME (LUKE 15:11–32)

The prodigal son story is a story for us today illustrating the journey home to Father and the acceptance of our rightful place as sons. Through the story, Jesus taught us about what the Father was really like and what keeps us from experiencing His love and our full inheritance as sons. One of the boys loses his inheritance because of looking for his life in worldliness, and the other loses his sonship through thinking like a slave.

SMALL GROUP ACTIVITY:

Read Luke 15:11–32.

How does this story illustrate the principle of stepping into our sonship as a journey? What obstacles do you see in both sons? What do you learn about the Father in the story?

In this pectoral tale, you have several actors. First, there is the father who is so gracious, kind, and loving. He is not some cosmic pushover, and yet he never treats these boys like they deserve. In fact, he gives them the very opposite of what they deserve. He is a father of grace and utter goodness. Second, there is the younger son who asks for his inheritance and then squanders it on prostitutes and riotous living. Third, there are the servants of the father that you get glimpses of throughout the story. Last, there is the older brother who although faithful to the father as a servant had forgotten that he was a son and paid a terrible price for it. Let's pick up the story.

THE YOUNGER BROTHER

The younger brother took his inheritance and left the restrictive control of home to go do his own thing. However, when he realized he had wasted all his inheritance, was starving, and working on a pig farm, he was devastated. He remembered that back at his father's house, there was always more than enough, even for the servants there. His father was so good, that even the servants lived a blessed life! As the younger brother concocted His plan of return, he knew for sure that things could never be the same. He could never return to his father's house as a son because he had utterly dishonored his father and completely blown his share of the inheritance. This could only mean one thing, their father-son relationship was over, just as if he had died. He decided that it would be better to be a servant in his father's house than die out in the far country. Through his own words, you can see that the son was ashamed of his behavior and sorry for his actions. He thought his father could never take him back as a son, but surely would take him back as a servant. He really didn't plan it as a journey home but as a relocation to a better master. He could never have his home again with his father because of the way he lived.

There was no way the son could not have ever foreseen how the father would react. Oh, but the Father Jesus is talking about is different. No, not different; OTHER, completely OTHER. He's unlike any of us. He lives and operates from a whole different set of values, a different form of life and love that had never been seen before.

How many times do we as Christians fall into this same trap—choosing to sin and then thinking we will have to earn our Father God's love back again just like a servant? This way of thinking is moving from the spirit of adoption back into the spirit of bondage. And that breaks the heart of our loving Father. He waits for us to repent of sin and then return to our intimate relationship with Him.

THE FATHER'S SHOCKING RESPONSE

What was taking place back home while the son was out throwing away his inheritance and making a mockery of his father? The father had been watching and waiting for his son to come home. The father longed for the estranged, sinful son to find the journey back to him. Then one day, his diligent watch was rewarded. When the father saw the sad figure of his son, slunk shouldered, smelling to high heaven in the distance, HE RAN! Yes, he ran to him to welcome him back home. These were older boys in their 30s probably according to Jewish culture making the dad somewhere in his 50s or 60s. Just picture this old man, hiking up his robe and sprinting down the road with dust flying off his sandals! When he gets to his son, Scripture records he throws himself on the smelly, dirty, wicked-hearted young man and cannot stop kissing him. Yes, kissing him. What kind of father is this? Have YOU met the Father—this Father?

As the son gave his plea to the father to allow him to come back not as a son, but as a servant, the father did something that's hard to believe. He wouldn't even let the disgraced boy call himself a slave and welcomed him home as a SON! "The LORD is gracious and full of compassion, Slow to anger and great in mercy" (Psalm 145:8 NKJV).

The father doesn't stop there, he begins to bless the boy with all of the rights and privileges of sonship as if he'd never sinned! Oh, what a father. Let's catch Jesus's revelation He's unfolding here. Let's look at what the father gave that day and what our Father still gives us today:

- *The Best Robe: In Jesus's day, the robe symbolized a change of identity and a clean appearance in the eyes of the Father and the eyes of the household. When he had his servant place a new robe upon the filthy prodigal, the father was saying, "I'm washing away your shame and giving you a fresh start with a clean, new identity!" But Jesus didn't say a new robe; He said the best robe. What was He saying? I am giving you the very best, the highest, the most beautiful identity anyone could ever have and you have to do nothing for it. Just come home! You can't earn it, and you don't get "cleaned up" to receive it. It's my identity and I bestow it upon you.*

- *The Family Ring of Authority: This was not just any ring, it was most likely the signet ring of the father representing the authority and wealth of the father himself. It carried the family seal. It was like the family bank card with the authority to carry out family business without limitations. If I was the father, I would have let him serve me awhile and prove himself, but not this father! He immediately gave the son the right to use the family name and authority to get back into life and work. Can't you imagine the servants watching this thinking, "He's crazy! This is the one who squandered everything and he gave him the family ring. What's he thinking?" I'll tell you what he's thinking, we are no longer slaves but sons, with the full rights, privileges, and authority as sons. When? NOW!*

- *The Sandals of Sonship: In the middle eastern culture of Jesus's day, slaves went barefoot, but never a son. In every house there was a distinction between servant/*

slave and son and the sandals of honor were one of these signs. Somewhere along the way, the boy had lost his sandals and walked and lived like the poorest of slaves. BUT NOT IN THIS FATHER'S HOUSE! The sandals of honor were symbols of the son's restored position. The father would not have his son walking around looking like some common slave. He restored him to the full rights of sonship immediately. These sandals were a sign to the son that he was not a servant, but a child of honor.

THE OLDER BROTHER: A SLAVE LIVING IN THE FATHER'S HOUSE

This story is really about two brothers from two different worlds and one very, very good father. In fact, this father is almost too good to believe. But we must believe. The younger brother represents for us a son who makes his way home into sonship from the world. He's the worldly son. The older brother, on the other hand, represents the religious or the church son. The one who never left the father's house, but somehow lost his way right in the midst of it. Let's take a look at this older brother. Be careful, you might just see yourself in the midst of this second half of the tale.

As the older brother walked in that late afternoon from the field, he was greeted with the sound of music and the smell of a Texas-sized barbecue going on up at the father's house. One of the servants met him along the way and said something like, "I can't believe it. He came home and your father's overjoyed! He even killed the calf you were fattening up for the big feast later on in the spring!"

The older brother did not rejoice that his brother had returned, because he was overwhelmed with what he saw as the unfairness of the situation. The saddest part of this story is that although the older brother had lived and worked with the father for years, he never saw the father's heart or his true nature! He thought of his father as a tough master who was hard to please, who seldom rewarded good work or behavior. Here are some things we see in the older brother:

- *He was jealous the father restored and celebrated his younger brother purely by grace and didn't give him what he deserved.*

- *He was focused on his own obedience to his father's every command, ("Look, these many years I have served you, and I never disobeyed your command") which spoke of self-righteousness! When we rejoice more in our own works or commitment to God rather than God Himself as our Father, we are trusting in our own self-righteousness.*

- *He lived like a poor servant, ("You never even gave me a young goat, that I might celebrate with my friends.") although he had already been given his larger share of the inheritance as a free gift of sonship at the very beginning of the saga. Go back and read the first two verses yourself. The boy was a millionaire but lived like a squatter! He was enjoying none of it because he was still trying to earn it through slavish hard work.*

- *Above all he didn't know the father, he only knew the master!*

THE FATHER'S SHOCKING RESPONSE: PART 2

> *"And he [the father] said to him, 'Son, you are always with me, and all that is mine is yours. It was fitting to celebrate and be glad, for this your brother was dead, and is alive; he was lost, and is found.'"*

> *Luke 15:31 ESV*

Every time I read these words, I cannot help but rejoice in that I'm convinced our Father is saying these same things to us. Let's look into the father's response to his religious, legalistic son who had lost the plot of the sonship story and had reduced himself to living as a beggar slave right in the midst of the father's house.

- *"Son"*: At first glance, this looks appropriate and normal except that Jesus did not use the word for a mature son, huios, that should have been used. Jesus used the word teknon, which is used for a very young child that hasn't reached any form of maturity, perhaps five to seven years old. Why in the world would Jesus do this? Why would the father in His story use this word? Simple, he was calling out to something deep inside the young man that had been lost—you're my boy! He was in essence saying, "You forgot who you were. Remember when we used to go fishing and when you'd lay your head on my shoulder at night and ask me to tell you a story. Remember when we played ball together, and watched movies? Remember, you're my son!"

- *"You are always with me"*: This is the only time in the Scripture I can recall these words spoken like this. Most often it is God, our Father, saying that HE is always with us! But again, that's not how Jesus says it coming out of the father's mouth in the closing lines of this story. Why? He was making a point about sonship—a son always has complete and unfettered access to the Father. "You are always, yes always, always with me! You have access to me all the time and in the most intimate ways, but you've forgotten to use it. You moved out of my house and are living in the barn like a servant. Come back in the house son, for you are always with me!"

- This last line is high impact. It's a revelation that if we get it, everything changes—yes, everything! "All that is mine is yours." The father was reaffirming what he had done in the first words of the story where it says he divided his wealth between them. In the Jewish world, the older brother received a double portion. He was immensely rich from the very beginning but because of his slave's mentality, he had lived like a pauper! Listen again with the ears of faith, "All that is Mine is yours!" What would happen if we believed these words? What would happen if we learned to access the Father's wealth and use it for His Kingdom's good? Everything, yes everything, would change!

In these three final statements we find the essence of living as a son—an intimate relationship, constant, unfettered access, and

THE JOURNEY HOME | 62

glorious riches beyond our wildest dreams. What would happen if these three things were the foundations of our lives? What would happen if we got these three truths so deep in our spirits that they were the beginning place of all of our thoughts?

An interesting side note is that Jesus told this story to the religious leaders who were grumbling about His love and fellowship with those they felt were sinners. "Now the tax collectors and sinners were all drawing near to hear him. And the Pharisees and the scribes grumbled, saying, 'This man receives sinners and eats with them.' So he told them this parable" (Luke 15:1–3 ESV). The story was aimed at them, and they would have easily known that He considered them the "older brothers" in the tale. The amazing ending is this: we don't know if the religious son who lived like a slave ever came home to the father. He chose not to finish the story on purpose. Was He perhaps saying that the journey into true, genuine sonship is more difficult for the legalistic son than the worldly one? Perhaps!

But the star of this story is not the younger son who came home, but the father. The story is far more about an unbelievably good father who offers sonship with every conceivable privilege by grace. This is OUR Father, the Father of Jesus, the Father of glory. We simply must make the journey into sonship. Let's not get lost along the way.

APPLICATION:

How will this Father/son relationship change your life? What three things will you practically begin to do today based upon what you have learned?

PART TWO

THE RELATIONAL JOURNEY INTO FATHERHOOD AND MOTHERHOOD

This journey into becoming spiritual fathers and mothers doesn't begin with doing something or even trying to take on a certain kind of lifestyle. It begins with realizing our own place as children in a great Father's house then beginning to live from that wonderful, life-altering relationship. When we begin to hear the Father say, "You are My beloved son/daughter, in you I am well pleased," then the journey home has truly begun. We've entered the Father/Son Paradigm!

The entire first section of this booklet was about realizing this elemental spiritual reality and beginning to live from there. In this second section, we will shift our focus to the second aspect of this paradigm—living as fathers and mothers to the next generation bringing forth mature sons and daughters who engage this world with a furious heart of mercy and faith.

Get ready for the wild ride ahead!

CHAPTER SEVEN

LET'S LOOK AT THE PRACTICAL SIDE

In the early years of our marriage, Callie and I lived in a small central Texas town where I coached ninth grade football and taught crazy teenagers at the local middle school. These were exciting years for us as we were beginning the journey of life together and trying to figure out how to do this thing Jesus called the Kingdom of God.

Our church was 45 miles away in a larger city and every member went to a home group near their home. Our group met in a location between our home and the church, and you would expect us to be in a group for young couples, but no, not the Boyds. We do everything backwards. Our group leaders were a retired couple named Ruben and Donna, and most of the members were older than 40! Wow, we were an outlier. Ruben and Donna weren't really teachers of the Bible, they couldn't sing, and sometimes the meetings didn't exactly flow smoothly. In spite of their weaknesses as group leaders, the group continually grew and multiplied itself—over and over and over!

What was this elderly couple's secret, their magic ingredient? Well, they listened really well. They believed that each of us had God's hand upon us in a special way. They gave the ministry away and encouraged each of us like crazy. They were always available, always willing, always loving, always, always, always—like a father and mother. That was their secret, they weren't picture perfect leaders, but they were great at being a father and a mother in the things of Jesus and His Kingdom. That was their magic ingredient, their secret sauce.

At the same time that Ruben and Donna were helping us grow up through the power of relationship, we met Tommy, the pastor from the neighboring city whom I spoke about at the beginning of this booklet. These two influences became a compelling springboard for the course of our lives—we would use the power of relational ministry as the Kingdom power tool to change the world. I look back today and am so, so grateful to the Father for placing this couple in our lives at the very onset of our Kingdom journey.

SPIRITUAL FATHERING: A DEFINITION

So here we go, it's time to try to give a definition to this. Spiritual fathering and mothering is . . . Are you ready? Drum roll please! Doing something on purpose on a regular basis to help the emerging generations grow up and be successful. Let's look at this amazingly deep definition of spiritual fathering and mothering.

- *Doing Something: I know you want a much deeper, clearer, and more profound beginning to this definition but this is it—doing something! Why don't I give you a formula for total success? It's simple, because life is NOT that way. Formulas work in science, but they are terrible in relational life and ministry. Formulas leave those I serve feeling like a project, and rightfully so, for that's what they are—my project—if I approach them in a formulaic manner. As a father and mother, there are a million "somethings" you do along the way to help your natural children grow up and be successful. You do what the moment, the stage of maturity, and the situation calls for. Being a father or mother is a whole lot more about living with your eyes and ears wide open and responding to the moment to insert that missing ingredient for maturity in that divinely open moment. So the beginning of all fathering and mothering is doing something.*

- *On Purpose: Many who want to disciple others, and*

even aspire to become a great father or mother to the coming ones, just hang out and listen. They are available, but they don't do something on purpose. So what is the purpose? To see them grow up and mature in Christ and lead a successful life in His Kingdom. Listen to our teacher Paul, "Him we proclaim, warning everyone and teaching everyone with all wisdom, that we may present everyone mature in Christ. For this I toil, struggling with all his energy that he powerfully works within me" (Colossians 1:28–29 ESV). The fatherly apostle had a purpose—to bring everyone around him into maturity in Jesus Christ. He doesn't just hang out and hope Jesus does something along the way. He does things on purpose to help his sons and daughters to grow up into Christ and into successful people.

- On a Regular Basis: This next idea of our definition speaks of an ongoing relationship that comes together regularly and lasts for some time. Most of us in service to Jesus and His people have become event based and no longer use the power of regular, long-term relationships as one of the power tools of heaven. I'm sorry, but good fathers and mothers don't live from event to event. They are in it for the long haul on a daily, interactive basis. They are not leaving. They desire ongoing, regular, consistent interaction so that they might invest into the lives of their sons and daughters.

- To Help Emerging Generations: What is this about emerging generations? Does that mean that we have to be 50 years old and work with 20-somethings? No, not at all. I'm speaking of the up and coming in Jesus regardless of age. When I was 34, I was mentoring and discipling men in their 40s. When we opened this ministry in the nations, I was 39 years old and began to mentor and father men in their 50s, and at times 60s. So what's the truth here? I'm one or two steps ahead in Christ and in His Kingdom ways, and I reach back to anyone who is hungry, available, and moldable, and say, "Come on, let's do this thing together for a season and I'll do my best to help you grow along the way." I'm convinced that many who are streaming into the Body of Christ in the nations of the earth (regardless of age) are hoping for someone to look over their *shoulder in this Kingdom Race and say, "Hey, come on, let me show you the way!"*

- *Grow Up: Let's look back to Paul's statement above about His purpose stated so plainly in Colossians 1:28 (ESV): "that we may present everyone mature [complete; full; wanting nothing; perfect], in Christ." This describes a clear goal—perfect, fully mature, wanting nothing, full, etc. That's our goal in this thing. That's why we are in this business of becoming a spiritual father or mother, to see sons and daughters grow up into full and perfect maturity. That would include things like learning to love Him and the world, believing Him and His promises, making good decisions on a daily basis, hearing His voice and following it, and approaching daily life through a value and belief system that has come from above. Simple, let's just help them grow up in all things in Him.*

- *And Become Successful: In the early days of trying to learn to disciple others and live as a spiritual papa to them, I made sure I kept everything spiritual, very spiritual. "Don't bother me with your marriage or your job, or those mundane everyday life things! We have to talk about the deep things of following Jesus!" Boy, did I have a lot to learn. Fathers and mothers don't just want their kids to be close to Jesus. They want that closeness with Him to translate into everyday living making their kids successful, healthy members of society representing Him in the mundane everyday life! I'll never forget when our children, Josiah, Bethany, and Hannah, were small. The Father showed us a guiding text to raise our kids: "The LORD was with Joseph, and he became a successful man" (Genesis 39:2 ESV). This became our parental goal—to cultivate a life in our children that the Lord would be clearly with them and His witness would create a life of success in all the daily life areas. If that's the heart of a Mom and Dad in the natural realm, shouldn't that be our heart in the spiritual realm also? Shouldn't we have such influence that marriages are healthy and happy, that finances are blessed and used with purpose, that employees are successful, that businesses are blessed, and that the world is deeply influenced by the happy, successful people of God serving and bringing His blessing to others?*

A FATHER IN A T-SHIRT

Over our years of service in Kenya, I began to notice a ministerial distance between pastors and spiritual leaders and the everyday believers in the local churches. There was deep honor and respect toward the godly leaders Jesus had brought into the congregations and there was genuine love for the people in the hearts of leaders, but there was this, this distance!

On one of our trips, we were holding a pastors/leaders conference near Mount Kenya and after the day of training ended, we were having tea in one of the pastor's homes. It was a wonderful moment with about 10 of us and there was healthy laughter and joy in what Jesus had done among us that day. Toward the end of our fellowship together, an older Kenyan gentleman entered and the atmosphere in the room shifted. He had such joy and a rapport with the other younger pastors I had not noticed in my years of working within the land. Our host began to share about how he and his wife had lived with this man's family in the beginning days of ministry. Another shared a similar story, and each of them began to recite account after account of how this brother had been a father to them and how this man's home was the very source of life they found in the early days of learning to serve Jesus.

After these glowing introductions, myself and this father sat and chatted. He laughed at the stories and simply said something like, "Isn't that Jesus's way? Didn't He open His life and not just His Bible?" As we talked further, he recounted, with a hearty chuckle, the story of 10 young men and women he and his wife were discipling a few years back in their home. The first little get together was a shock to the young, Kenyan believers— he wore blue jeans and a T-shirt! Finally, the awkwardness was broken by a young lady when she stated, "We didn't know that pastors ever wore 'normal clothes.' We thought they always wore their 'ministry suit.'" We lamented over this funny observation by these young people. They had never been with a leader who had taken off his ministry suit and was just a plain man, a plain father!

Isn't it time to become like this Kenyan father in the faith and lay down our ministry suits, step out from behind our pulpits and meetings, and let the younger ones into our homes and lives as we simply wear a T-shirt?

WE'VE BEEN BLESSED

Callie and I have been so blessed to have a host of spiritual fathers, mothers, mentors, and guides in our life. It all began with our own biological parents. They were great examples, coaches, friends, and disciplinarians when needed. Callie and I could not have been more blessed! Then, as I began my coaching career, Buster and Becky came into our lives. Buster was a head football coach I served under, and Becky was an amazing wife and mother. Wow, they mothered and fathered us in Jesus, in all those seeming early crises when you have your first children, and how to navigate a healthy balance of family, faith, and career. What did we ever do to deserve them? In the midst of life, there has always been Jackie and Linda, our pastor and his wife. When I was fired from my first ministry attempt and we lost a baby in the process, they were there. When that magical moment occurred for me to leave the coaching profession behind and step into a vocational ministry role, voila, they were there. As I began to form Prepare International into a viable force for Jesus, they have been there every step of the way. I could go on and on about Alan and Eileen and Jack and Friede, but you get the point. Every step of our way, our good and kind heavenly Father has had a father and mother with skin on, to be His representative and His hands, mouth, voice, eyes, and ears. Should we NOT pass that blessing along? Shouldn't we become the Jackie and Linda or Buster and Becky for the young ones Jesus is calling to Himself?

THE CHURCH NEEDS AN ORPHANECTOMY

Jack Taylor, one of the most marvelous spiritual Papa's heaven has ever sculpted tells us all the time, "The Kingdom of God is a family! If He wanted it to be anything else, He would have never told us to say 'OUR FATHER'"! Calling Him Father makes this a family business and beginning that prayer with "our Father" connects us all together in His great house. If we are a family, we should act like it. I've heard him say over and over something of the sort, "the religious system we've come out of has been more of an orphanage than a family. We all need an orphanectomy!" Not sure about that word, but it sure does seem right. We need an orphanectomy—the removal of the orphan heart and orphan mind from each of our lives and our ministries! The only possible outcome could be a massive movement of fathers and mothers giving their lives to love and mature the emerging ones in Jesus. Come on! Let's do it!

Chapter Eight

AND THE WINNER IS?

As we carry on in this journey of discovery in the Father/Son Paradigm, let's take a peek into the lives of two of the great fathers in Scripture, Abraham of the Old and Barnabas of the New. These men found both the heart and the capacity to bring forth Kingdom carriers through their fathering efforts. What can we learn from these men? What can we carry into our daily lives? Well, let's jump in and discover.

ABRAHAM

Abraham is a strange duck! I teach an entire 8–10 hour course on his life as the prototype man of the Kingdom of God and I'll try not to bore you with all the details. Did you ever wonder why God chose Abraham out of the midst of a terribly idolatrous generation? Was it his piety? His great holiness? His deep reverence and obedience? No, that all comes later. Scripture is very, very clear why Abraham was chosen to be His Kingdom man, His Kingdom prototype. In fact, no other Old Testament believer or follower of the Lord is pointed to as the prime example we are to follow. Abraham's the guy! Listen to Paul, "What then shall we say that Abraham our father has found . . . [The blessing comes to those] who also walk in the steps of the faith which our father Abraham had . . . And if you are Christ's, then you are Abraham's seed, and heirs according to the promise" (Romans 4:1,12; Galatians 3:29 NKJV). David was awesome. Yet we are never told to follow his footsteps of faith or that he is our father. We could say the same of Moses, Elijah, Samuel, or Joseph. The list goes on and on. Why Abraham? Why did God choose him in the midst of an idol worshiping world? Why is HE and HE ONLY the example and father of our faith?

· Listen to the clearly stated words of the Lord as to why Abraham was chosen out of the multitudes of his day, "For I have chosen him, that he may command his children and his household after him to keep the way of the LORD by doing righteousness and justice, so that the LORD may bring to Abraham what he has promised him" (Genesis 18:19 ESV). Wow, rocket science! He was chosen because of his amazing faith? No. He was chosen because of his supernatural abilities? No. He was chosen because of his unswerving obedience? Have you even read his story? It was simple: He was chosen to be a father who would pass on all that he accumulated in his heart and soul from heaven to his children. I love the New Living Translation version of this text, "I have singled him out so that he will direct his sons and their families to keep the way of the LORD by doing what is right and just. Then I will do for Abraham all that I have promised." It's as if God is saying, "I have singled him out, yes, out of the millions, because somewhere in him, I see the ability to be a father who can pass it on, impart it, and transfer all I give him into the next generation! He has the IT factor! He's not just a father, he's a spiritual father!"

I've heard others speak on this passage before, but they never come to the end. The WHY behind God's choice of Abraham. We know He chose him because somewhere within, he could father and pass it on, but is that the big WHY of the whole deal? God just wants fathers who pass it on? Although this is critical, it's not the final big WHY. Listen to the end of the text, "so that the LORD may bring to Abraham what he has promised him." This is enormous. The implication of these words is that God is able to fully keep all that is in His heart and all that He has promised IF, and only if, Abraham becomes a healthy father who imparts faith and the Kingdom way into his sons. If Abraham cannot pass it on, if he doesn't rise to the challenge of being an impartational spiritual father, then God will NOT fulfill all of His promises to Abraham. So herein lies a life-altering, game-changing Kingdom principle:

- *Where God finds impartational, Kingdom-transferring spiritual mothers and fathers, THERE He pours out the fullness of His promises. THERE He reveals Himself in faithfulness. THERE He radically and more fully empties heaven of its great treasures into the earth!*

Listen to the last report of Abraham's life, "Abraham gave everything he owned to his son Isaac. But before he died, he gave gifts to the sons of his concubines and sent them off" (Genesis 25:5–6 NLT). That phrase, "Abraham gave everything . . . to his son Isaac," speaks volumes. The story isn't just speaking of sheep, goats, cattle, and wells. It is booming much, much more. Abraham was able to impart faith, reverence, deep love, loyalty, and the Kingdom way of *El Elyon*, God Most High, the true and living God, who had revealed himself to this old man many years before. And upon the death of Abraham, Scripture declares, "After Abraham's death, God blessed his son Isaac" (Genesis 25:11 NLT). The hand and blessing of God that was upon a father's life was immediately transferred to the son and the story continued. The mighty rushing river of the Kingdom of God continued on in a son. Then again in Jacob and again in Joseph until this family both "saved" the world and sat on its throne in mighty ruling power and authority. Fathering saves; mothering grants ruling authority. It is the very operating system of the Kingdom of God.

BARNABAS

Our New Testament champion is Barnabas. He's not spoken of in volumes, but his impact was enormous. We first find him in Acts 4 when many were selling property and laying the proceeds at the feet of the apostles. In this opening story, we discover his given name was Joseph, but the Twelve knew him well and had nicknamed him Barnabas, which either means son of encouragement or son of prophecy. Well, I guarantee you, no one will ever nickname me that! When Saul of Tarsus, the great persecutor of the Church, was converted and later found his way back to Jerusalem where he had helped launch the initial onslaught of persecution, most were gravely afraid of him and held him at arm's length. Not Barnabas. He began to spend time with the young convert and became convinced that he had genuinely met Jesus, and Jesus had done a great miracle in the young man. He brought him to the apostles who began to get to know him only to have Paul begin a second round of problems due to his lack of wisdom, but this time on the Kingdom side. They sent the young firebrand away so that peace could return to the Church.

Later, as the great revival breaks out in Antioch, the apostles send Barnabas, the son of encouragement and prophecy, down to pastor the mighty move. When he arrives and surveys the scene, we have one of the great, but hidden texts of the New Testament, "So Barnabas went to Tarsus to look for Saul, and when he had found him, he brought him to Antioch. For a whole year they met with the church and taught a great many people. And in Antioch the disciples were first called Christians" (Acts 11:25–26 ESV). Barnabas sees the situation and then goes and finds young Saul of Tarsus, who had been cast off and discarded by the Twelve! Wow. What a verse! "So Barnabas went to look for Saul, and when he had found him, he brought him [back]." Under the tutelage and fathering of Barnabas, Saul is transformed into Paul (meaning little or small!). I've heard it said, "Without Barnabas, we have no Paul!"

Barnabas later does the same thing with a second young man, John Mark. On Paul's and Barnabus's first missionary journey, John Mark was their apprentice and helper. While on the island of Crete, a persecution broke out and John Mark leaves them, probably out of fear, and heads home to Jerusalem. Later, as they begin preparations for a second journey, Barnabas desires to take John Mark again, giving him a second chance, but Paul would have nothing of it. He chooses Silas, and Barnabas again goes and finds Mark in Jerusalem and then heads back to Crete to begin their journey together. It seems Barnabas was always going and finding great young men that had failed and been cast off by others and invested in them until they became Kingdom shakers and world changers. I love the statement about taking him back to Crete! Why Crete? What's the significance? That's where John Mark had abandoned them on the first journey. It was the place of his great failure. Barnabas took the boy to face his failure, to face himself, to find hope and courage and dignity again, and the rest is history! We have a book of the Bible because of that!

It seems this man had an ocean size capacity to father others. I believe the key is within his nickname. As the son of prophecy, he could see the hidden potential that lay within the young broken ones and the failures that others had cast off, and he would go and find them! As the son of encouragement, he constantly spoke hope, life, destiny, and faith until they eventually left his side and became radical Kingdom carriers. Oh, that we could become like Barnabas. Oh, that we could see into the young ones. That we would go and find them. That we would speak life transforming encouragement until they went out mature and full of Christ and His Kingdom.

So what is Barnabas's legacy? His fathering gave us the mighty Apostles Paul and John Mark. But it goes much further than this. 62% of the entire New Testament text is connected to his fathering efforts through Paul, John Mark, and later Luke. 16 of these golden books of revelation and wisdom came to us as a result of this spiritual papa! Now, that's a legacy. Yes, that's the power of fathering!

So you decide. Who's the champion? Who takes the prize: Abraham or Barnabas? Well, I think it's too soon to decide. The story is still being written. Maybe it will be YOU!

SMALL GROUP DISCUSSION:

With a group, discuss what you learned through the lives of Abraham and Barnabas. How did Abraham give all that he had to Issac? How can you? How can you become more like Barnabas as both the son of encouragement and the son of prophecy?

What is the importance of this principle we learned, "Where God finds impartational spiritual mothers and fathers, THERE He pours out the fullness of His promises. THERE He reveals Himself in faithfulness. THERE He radically and more fully empties heaven of its great treasures into the earth!"

CHAPTER NINE

REMOVING THE OBSTACLES

Any time you try to make a change in your life or within a group, there are always obstacles. There is an old saying but it's still true today, "Change happens when the pain of staying the same is greater than the pain of change." I pray the Lord will put His kind and loving but very firm pressure upon each until every obstacle is cast aside and many begin this journey of becoming fathers and mothers in the Kingdom of God.

OBSTACLES MANY FACE IN THIS JOURNEY

Ignorance: Many have only experienced organizational, program-based Christianity. They don't know anything different. Perhaps you thought that better programs, better sermons, or more anointing was the key, but in reality, the key is Jesus's relational ministry style—fathering. Each of us has no more excuses. The Bible is full of examples, and together, we are discovering a new way of making disciples bringing others into maturity.

Selfishness: Selfishness is a second obstacle that many face. It is much easier just to teach a class or lead a home group meeting than to give your life as a father or mother to others. Most people really don't want their compartmentalized lives disturbed. They only have so much time for God and His Kingdom's people. To be a teacher, a home group leader, or a pastor is one level of commitment—you can turn it on and off, but to be a father or mother costs you much more. You can't turn it off. They are always there, always available, always fathers, always mothers.

Busyness: Many are so wrapped up in busy lifestyles that they miss the important things of God's Kingdom realm. The busyness of the world often results in an apathy toward becoming what we see we should become. Even being busy with spiritual work doesn't mean you will have any reward in heaven. Perhaps, you are busy with the wrong spiritually-oriented activities. Perhaps, you have bought into a lie and are doing things every day that Jesus never asked you to do. Let's not fall prey to the trap of busyness with the lesser things that we miss a life in the Father/ Son Paradigm.

Insecurity and Fear: Maybe you are filled with fear and insecurity. Perhaps you say to yourself, "I don't know enough; I have had no good role models," or "I've never even had a spiritual father or mother." Join the club! When you become a natural parent, do you really know what to do? No! The job is thrust upon you, and you learn in the midst of doing. You are never perfect and you make mistakes, but somehow God uses you to raise children that love and serve Him. You don't have the luxury of waiting until you arrive at some magical, heavenly maturity level in God to begin being a spiritual parent. The amazing thing about God is that He takes each of us where we are at and begins a work through us if we are simply willing. The Lord is waiting for you to stand up and offer yourself to be used—even if you have a long way to go and a lot to learn. Don't we all?

No Long-Term Kingdom Vision: Many don't enter this great work of the Father/Son Paradigm because they have no long-term Kingdom-oriented vision. All they see is their family, their job, ministry, or church. They never see that fathering keeps the Kingdom moving into the next generation and turns one into a multiplier. This short-sightedness was a weakness of many in Bible days, including King Hezekiah.

In 2 Kings 20:13–19, King Hezekiah betrays the fact that he had no long-term vision for the Kingdom of God. Isaiah prophesied that things would be at peace during the king's life, but that the next generation would have hardship, trial, and the people of God would be overrun by their enemies. In verse 19 the king is recorded as saying, "'The word of the LORD you have spoken is good. For he thought, 'Why not, if there will be peace and security in my days?'" (ESV) How in the world could this prophetic word be good?

All the king could see was his ministry and his lifetime. He had lost sight of God, and of anything other than himself and his own generation. Only through raising up the next generation of the servants of Christ can we keep the Kingdom moving powerfully forward and multiply what God has given us into future generations.

Hurts From the Past: One last thing that might be holding you back is a wound from the past. These hurts can take many forms, such as family hurts, spiritual abuse by authorities, or a past failure in life or ministry. It's time you let the past be the past and move on to do God's will! God will not allow your past to excuse you from bearing the Kingdom fruit of mature sons and daughters. There is no excuse because each of us can be made whole through Jesus Christ.

I'll never forget the pull of this temptation to allow wounds and hurts from the past to stop me from giving my life as a spiritual father. Several years ago, one of our closest spiritual sons turned on us and went back into the world. We were deeply wounded by his verbal and emotional attack against us, and he was again devastated by worldly decisions and sinful choices. Our hearts broke for him, but we were also broken deeply on the inside because of his turning away. Pain, real pain in this journey.

It WILL come, but we can't allow hurts of the past and pain in the journey to stop us. In fact, every obstacle this world and the evil one throws against us can either be a terrible obstacle or a wonderful stepping stone. Often, it's those who have borne the pain of life and come through who are the most marvelous, compassionate healers, fathers, mothers, mentors, and coaches.

I don't know what your obstacles are, but let's set them aside and embrace this fantastic life of investing in the emerging ones of the Kingdom of God. There's nothing like it!

CHAPTER TEN

FACES

Any of us who have raised children are well aware of this fact: one size DOES NOT FIT ALL. When our first child was born, little Josiah David, we realized everything we read in those wonderful parenting books and the class we took at church must have been written and taught by someone who had never even seen a kid, let alone raised one. About the time we got into a rhythm with him, along came Bethany. Wow, what a girl! But there was this problem—she was a girl, and the rules changed. And then one more, Hannah, the ultra girl. Everything changed with each child that God brought into our lives and then a terrifying thing happened—they would not stop growing, changing, and maturing which placed an unbelievable demand upon Callie and I to constantly evolve as parents. We realized one size does not fit all and one style does not fit the same child as they grow. We had to learn to wear many faces along the way.

In the same way, as you give yourself to living in the Father/ Son Paradigm as a Kingdom parent, you will discover that there are many faces you will have to wear along the journey. In the Greek theater world, there would only be a handful of actors in each play, most often only three, with all being male. Each of the three would take on multiple roles, including the roles of women in the script. How did they pull this off? They carried multiple masks, called *prosopa*, which literally meant face. The actors would switch masks, faces, back and forth, right before the spectators in order to live out the drama or comedy they were in. One actor playing multiple roles with a different face for each role—sounds like parenting, spiritual parenting.

These different faces we will explore describe different kinds of discipling or mentoring relationships we must take on in the process of helping the next ones grow and mature. Some of these relationships are very intense and deliberate, while others are of a more passive/reactive nature. Because of differing stages of maturity, personalities, life experiences, and the list goes on of those we father, we must wear a different face to bear fruit in their lives. Some of these roles (faces) are very deliberate and highly interactive, while others are more passive and reactive in nature.

MOST DELIBERATE: HANDS-ON ROLES

Discipler of a Young Christian: Every time a new baby arrived in our home, two things came with the child: great joy and a lot of hard work. Callie was a stunning mother from the beginning. It was as if the heavenly Father wove into the fabric of her psyche a constant download of what to do. Despite her giftedness, it was still super hands-on and very deliberate. A discipler of a new Christian is very similar to a parent with a new baby. A discipler of a new believer through consistent relationship shares his life and knowledge with the young believer so they can become stable and strong in Christ. When disciples are young believers, the relationship can, and probably should be very intense. The discipler is often the one who has to initiate the contact, direct the process, and feed the young ones. Besides all of this, he/she often has to clean up the messes of life as their "new baby" falls and fails along the way. Although this process can last up to a few years, by the end of this phase, the new believer should be weaned off of the deep need for an intense relationship and has learned to feed him/herself and follow Jesus in the daily areas of life.

Spiritual Guide: I'll never forget our vacation years ago hiking with friends in the Alps. There was this one hike that terrified me, yes I was scared spitless! The problem was that Bethany thought it was a stroll in the park. But, thank God we had a very experienced guide who looked me in the eye and said, "I know this path; I've been here many times before. Just trust me and I'll get you up to that peak." Without her help, I would have never made the ascent. Likewise, a spiritual guide helps maturing Christians discover <u>where they are</u> in the Lord and <u>how to move forward</u> because they have been there before. They are primarily concerned with the ongoing process of a person's life in Christ and the Holy Spirit. As people begin to move into new places spiritually, there is almost always a period of confusion, even fear, and a need for guidance. A spiritual guide who has been there before and knows the path can listen and discern what God is doing and give counsel on how to move forward. This is a critical fathering and mothering relationship. This type of mentoring could last a few months or up to a year or two.

Spiritual Coach: I was an American football coach for many years, so I know a little bit about coaching. It's a coach's job to help their players discover their gifts and talents, and put them to full use in conjunction with the rest of the team. Coaches help people discover their gifts and refine their skills. A spiritual coach comes into someone's life to help them develop the skills and abilities they need to succeed in the task the Lord and life itself have placed before them. The coach helps someone assess what they are called to do, where they are, and what their strengths and weaknesses are. They then help the disciple to grow in the skills, abilities, and anointing necessary for success. This can be an intense relationship, but it is not usually a long one. It can range in length from quite short to a year or two.

About 10 years ago, the Lord brought a young man into my life. He was about 30 years old and an executive at a very successful company. He was one of those followers of Jesus who seemed to find success in anything he put his hand to, but the problem was, he was very unsatisfied. As we shared lunch over and over, I began to sense he had a full-time vocational call to ministry upon his life. As I listened to what the Lord was doing in his heart and where the roots of this deep dissatisfaction came from, I began to share my feelings about his calling. Lights began to go on within him. I even went on to describe what I saw the Lord might be doing and how that might fit into the local church world. Within one year, he had left his job and entered that particular leadership ministry within a rapidly expanding local church. I had been a spiritual guide, but my role didn't end there. Once he had made the transition, he had 100s of new questions about the how-to's of his new role. Over time, we answered some of those questions together, while he found other answers within his own life in Jesus. I had transitioned into our relationship from being a spiritual guide to a spiritual coach. How fun is that? What a privilege! Well, the journey hasn't ended. That rumbling and stirring are again at work within him. You should hear our chats over coffee and lunch now. The best is yet to come!

MODERATELY INTENSE: MORE OCCASIONAL IN NATURE

Counselor: A counselor helps their friends understand what is happening within their hearts, minds, and lives, and then helps to find answers so growth and victory can occur. This is not to be a long-term relationship. It should last for weeks or up to a year. This is more of a reactional relationship in which someone comes to you in need. We must understand that we do not want people to continually need our counsel or to stay in a long-term counseling relationship. The goal is to get them through the situation or problem into growing health and success. There is a real danger of causing people to be "counseling junkies"—those who are constantly introspective, always discovering new problems, and coming to their counselor for the newest broken place in life. We must guard against people becoming addicted to our counseling and always seeing their problems, instead of Jesus. If there is one addiction we want to create, it is an addiction to Jesus Himself. But having said that, being a counselor to others in need is a highly important face we should wear along the way. Listening, asking questions, giving wisdom, and praying prayers of deliverance, healing, and breakthrough into our young sons and daughters is an honor and an all-important role we will play in the journey of many.

Teacher: Alan Vincent has played one of the greatest roles in my life in introducing me to the Kingdom of God and the life of faith. We had a healthy, love-filled relationship and I went to him many times for counsel. But, the real key was his teaching. As I sat in the crowds and heard Alan share Scripture 100s of times or spoke with him about the Word in his study, Jesus used him to change my life! Through teaching, we can disciple and mentor others, and at times, we don't even need to be close to them. This may simply be a congregational role you play from the pulpit, in a class, or a homegroup. It can be ongoing, but our greatest goal is to teach and inspire others to feed their own souls and connect with Christ personally. Although, sometimes teachers can make people dependent upon them instead of the Lord. This is not healthy fathering. Fathers and mothers teach in such a way that their children develop their own capacities to learn and grow. Let's follow that path.

LOW INTENSITY: MOST PASSIVE AND REACTIVE IN NATURE

Examples and Models: Modeling is one form of discipling we must never underestimate. These models may be people from history, in other parts of the world, or our own homes. When mentoring people through modeling, we may not have any direct contact with them, but they watch how we live and how we operate, and our lives become the model they desire to follow and emulate. But, I believe this principle: the closer they are to me, the more powerful my example can be. As a young leader, the Lord allowed me to work around Joe White, the Director of Kanakuk and Kanakomo Camps. Joe and I often spoke and it was always such a blessing, but his great contribution to my life was as an example. I saw into this man's family, leadership, and faith.

Watching Joe daily was one of the great building blocks of my life. He was an example, a model.

In the life of our children's growing up years, I would wear many faces in a single day. I would weave almost seamlessly from being a playmate, to a friend, to a teacher, to a coach, to a diaper changer and mess cleaner-upper, to a conflict resolution mediator, to a nourisher and Dad. Faces, so many faces. In this grand adventure called the Kingdom of God as we choose to grow as spiritual fathers and mothers, is it not the same? Sure it is. Now, let's put on our "Game Face(s)" and get in the game!

SMALL GROUP DISCUSSION:

Look back at the six mentoring/discipling faces above. Has anyone filled one of these roles in your life? Which of these types of mentoring relationships have you ever filled in the life of another? How could you weave in and out of many of them in a relationship you are serving as a father or mother?

CHAPTER ELEVEN

THE BIG WIN

I'll never forget building our first home. We were so excited to move back to the city we had met and married in, Lubbock, Texas. A young builder agreed to build a home for us and many people pulled out all the stops doing favors for us in the building process. It was a blast of a time! But you know what we didn't do? We did not get all excited, run out, and buy all the materials from start to finish and go out into the vacant piece of ground and begin to try to assemble them all. Nope. That's not what we did. We worked with an architect for two months going back and forth on a plan until we had the house we wanted—on paper. This brilliant young man produced a set of blueprints for us that did two things: on the front was a picture of what the finished product would look like and then within were the step-by-step plans on how to get there. I'll never forget looking at the front picture 100s of times during the process making sure that what we desired was really being built.

That's just where we need to begin in the Father/Son Paradigm lifestyle. What is the finished product we are going for? What does it look like? What's the picture we can go back to over and over in the process to make sure we are raising the right kind of people for the Lord? Let's slow down, take a step back, and try to picture the big goal, the big win of this thing. It's simple: SONS, mature sons of our Father in heaven! Now, wait a minute and let me explain. When I use that term, I am using it without reference to gender just as the New Testament does. Many times, especially in the writings of Paul, the New Testament calls the children of God, both male and female, sons. God has sons and some are in the body of a girl. Now, that is not to say that at times, the text of Scripture also uses the term sons and daughters, for it does, but overall, "sons" is the New Testament word for God's children and I'm convinced there is a plan of the Holy Spirit behind this genderless term.

So what IS a mature son? A mature son or daughter of God is simply someone who has said a resounding YES to the Lord Jesus Christ and is growing into His likeness. Simple isn't it? Yes, it's very simple; it's just impossible. Yes, I said impossible. Everything in the Kingdom of God is impossible, but don't drop the book in the fireplace just yet. I have read so many books on making disciples, mentoring, coaching, and fathering that I could probably furnish an entire public library, and sometimes, they make it so complicated and place so many requirements and responsibilities that I honestly get overwhelmed. Let's make it simple: a mature son is one who says YES to Jesus and begins to grow into His image. Simple!

YES: The life of a disciple of Jesus and this Kingdom has as its foundation a heart and lifestyle of surrender to Jesus and our Father. YES is at the core of everything. In our years of natural parenting, one of the guiding lights of our journey was helping our children find within their own hearts this YES attitude toward the Lord and then seeing it worked out practically in their everyday life. It wasn't always easy and there were plenty of bumps in the road, but our children live surrendered lives to the Father and have given their hearts to His work around the world. Today Josiah and Brandi, his wife, live in Poland as missionaries. Bethany and Boone, her husband, sold a lucrative business here in Lubbock, where they met and married, and left all to venture into deep South Texas (wow, that's another world for you!). They became missionaries serving as the only Anglo pastors in a Filipino church that we helped plant years ago. Hannah and

Nathan, her beau, live here in Lubbock, with Hannah on our staff at Prepare International, and Nathan serving Jesus in the business world being a bright light and witness. Yes. What a joy that they have all said YES.

We didn't teach them all of the Bible, the deep things of God, the mighty ways of world missions, etc., but we did help lead them into a personal YES that dominates their lives and decisions today. Our children often didn't date when all their friends were, simply because there weren't radical Jesus followers available. They didn't go to the places many young people did. They gave their lives in summer missions, sought Jesus daily, gave generously, and lived as a witness the best they knew how to daily. YES. This is the mark of a son.

But this yes should go deeper and wider as the days go on. This is the sign of maturity. Maturity isn't knowing everything about everything, as much as it is a YES to Jesus that grows week by week, month by month, deeper and wider. Deeper in the fact that there is an ever greater giving of our lives, our affections, our time, and our gifts and talents for Him and others. Wider simply means that this YES encompasses all the practical areas of daily life. There's nothing withheld from this YES to Jesus. This is your goal, your big win—helping others around you through the power of friendship and the Holy Spirit working through your friendship to come to a big YES to Jesus that dominates their everyday walking-around life. This is a mature son of God!

GROWING INTO HIS LIKENESS: SO WHAT DOES HE LOOK LIKE?

The second part of our little picture is to grow into His image—Christlikeness. We could list so many traits that we could again get very overwhelmed, so let's flip open our "Blueprint" and see a few things that can be guiding pictures for us into helping younger believers grow into Jesus's image. So here's the picture we will work from:

Devotion: The first thing I focus on as I spend time with younger followers of Jesus is to help them grow in their lives of devotion. Jesus was always sneaking away to be with His Father. His greatest love was the presence of His Father, and He lived a life of deep devotion by being with Him. This was the secret of His life and power, and it was the secret of His holiness and victory—secret devotion unto the Father. But it wasn't just prayer and secret communion, Jesus was massively devoted to the Father's written words, the Scriptures. It is no exaggeration to say that He had memorized the entire body of Scripture, the Old Testament, before He ever burst on the scene in ministry. That's 37 complete books (929 chapters and 23,145 verses) he had "eaten" until they were His words, not just His Father's. God didn't allow Jesus to take shortcuts either; He did it as a human being. What a life of devotion—secret devotion—to the Father. This is the beginning place of all fathering and mothering, and it's a critical element of growing into the image of Jesus for young and old followers alike. This is the very place He began with the Twelve. Listen to Mark 3:13–14 (ESV), "And he went up on the mountain and called to him those whom he desired, and they came to him. And he appointed twelve (whom he also named apostles) so that they might be with him and he might send them out." He chose twelve and gave them one overriding job—be with Me! If it worked for Jesus, it'll work for you and I. Now, I wish we could devote an entire section of this booklet to this one cornerstone of truth, but let me simply say this: let them do it their way! Don't try to make them just like you in this area. Some will be more drawn to Scripture, others to prayer, others still to worship and music, and others to fasting or solitude. The list of ingredients goes on, but the key is to help them find an ever-growing life of devotion, based upon their own unique wiring from heaven. It's how Jesus lived and it's how we live too.

Co-Mission: The second page of our image of Jesus's blueprints tells us that He was a man on a mission to redeem the world so that His Father's Kingdom could flood into our realm transforming it! At the end of His time here on earth, Jesus shared His mission with all of us. It's called the Great Commission or as I like to think of it, Co-Mission—His and ours! "And Jesus came and said to them, 'All authority in heaven and on earth has been given to me. Go therefore and make disciples of all nations, baptizing them in the name of the Father and of the Son and of the Holy Spirit, teaching them to observe all that I have commanded you. And behold, I am with you always, to the end of the age'" (Matthew 28:18–20 ESV). What a fantastic gift—we have the high honor of joining Him in His cosmic mission! As you father and mother the emerging ones, don't just help them to become "good Christians." Maturity is taking on His mission as our own, His calling as our own, His responsibility for the world as our own. Each of us will play a different part and carry out a different set of good works, but to be conformed into His image is to take on the Great Co-Mission as our mission.

Character: As we flip the page to page three of the heavenly blueprint of Christlikeness, we find the word character at the top of the page. Character is who you are when no one is looking. Character is that collection of inner traits which makes you who you are. When you look in the New Testament, it is pregnant with 100s of character traits that we are to put on. It's really quite overwhelming, so I'll choose three that typify Jesus Christ: purity, generosity, and servanthood. Jesus was pure in every way. Money didn't move Him, nor did illegal sexuality. He was not controlled by any lust, whether it be that drive for more money and things or some kind of out-of-bounds sexual experience. He was pure. His purity was not some forced holiness, but a genuine, joyful flow of saying "no" to things around Him because of His full "YES" to the Father. Purity. We need to help those we lead to find an ever-deepening and all-encompassing purity. The second word I've chosen is generosity. Remember John 3:16 (NKJV), "For God so loved the world that He gave His only begotten Son." Generosity of life is the outworking of a life lived in love. Model it, speak about it, encourage it, praise when you see it, but we must cultivate hearts and lives of generosity in the character sketch of those we disciple. Servanthood. This life trait is a critical addition to the heart and toolbelt of any follower of Jesus. Jesus said, "the Son of Man did not come to be served, but to serve and to give His life" (Mark 10:45 ISV). Serving is Jesus's way. Serving is His Spirit. Serving is His heart. Thus we must seek to encourage and enforce lives of servanthood in those we mentor. I am currently spending time with a young believer named John. He has had a very difficult road through life and has made some very poor decisions along the way. I love him. He reminds me of Jesus. I met him as he volunteered to come help me lay grass sod in our new backyard. Then, he volunteered to stain a small deck we had built. Every time we speak, he tells me of someone the Lord has laid on his heart and how he is reaching out to do good, to give, and to serve. John reminds me of Jesus. He serves!

Supernatural: This is a page that is left out of most spiritual mother's and father's sets of blueprints for their children in the Lord. In fact, this page has been left out of the very playbook of the Church for centuries and we are just now rediscovering it in the Gospels and Acts. This Kingdom is utterly supernatural because the King is! To disciple or mentor another and not point them to a life full of the Holy Spirit and moving in supernatural faith and gifts is illegal in the Kingdom of God. It is like going into a championship game with your star player who scores all the goals sitting on the bench drinking a coca-cola! Let's get the Holy Spirit back in the forefront of the game through demonstrating and pressing our young followers into the supernatural realm. Let's go back and read the book of Acts as if that is the only normal way to live in the Kingdom of God. Let's look back into the Gospels with Jesus as the real model of what our everyday lives can be like. We have made being Christlike only about character and not about power. Shame on us! That wasn't Jesus's way with His early young sons in the faith. Jesus modeled the supernatural life and gifts, He moved in it daily, He encouraged His young followers to do the same, even correcting them when they did not. The supernatural is the natural way of the Kingdom. We must father like Jesus did, making the supernatural realm of the Spirit a normal page in our playbooks of mothering and fathering.

Love of His Body: The last page is the heart of so much, it's love. Love for the Body of Christ around us. So many love their church, or their denomination, or their particular brand of Christianity, but that's not enough. As we mentor, disciple, and raise up new believers in Jesus, we must help them see the entire Body as His and help them to love His Body as He does. We must put an end to this sectarianism and religious competition, and bring forth a new breed of Jesus followers who passionately and compassionately love His Body in all of its forms, colors, and creeds. But we can't let this be a mere sentimentality, it has to also be lived out in deep community with a local expression of believers. We've seen so many who preach and proclaim their love of the Body yet have no deep, accountable connections. Let's put into the souls of our spiritual children a sincere love and life in the local body of Christ while we also instill a deep love for His entire Body with all of its' shapes, sizes, colors, and beliefs.

When we moved into that house I spoke of after six to seven months of building, we were elated—we had built a house and it looked so much like the picture on the front of the blueprints our young architect friend had drawn for us. We were overjoyed! Isn't that what John meant when he wrote, "I have no greater joy than to hear that my children are walking in the truth" (3 John 1:4 ESV). The greatest joy of this old father's heart was to see his children (Do you hear the sound of the Father/Son Paradigm at work in John's words?) walking in the truth. What is the truth? Jesus said He was. I am the truth. When John looked at those who were coming in the next generation behind him that he was helping along the way and saw them maturing into sons and daughters that looked like Jesus, He was elated! That's the goal, the big win—mature sons. Sons and daughters of the Father who have a BIG YES at the core of their heart toward Him and are growing into the likeness of His Son. The Big Win!

CHAPTER TWELVE

MATURITY: JOURNEY OR DESTINATION?

When I was growing up, we drove a lot as a family. Our grandparents lived 100s of miles away and twice a year we would load up in the family sedan and take off across the country. My dad always wanted to get there and unfortunately, I've discovered that I'm cut out of the same cloth. The fun really didn't begin until we arrived at our destination because the journey was the necessary evil. Wow, was I in for a shock when I married Callie! At the end of our first year of marriage, Callie and I traveled halfway across the U.S. with her mom and dad. About halfway through the first day of driving, we began to pull off the road to read historical markers and have picnics. "What's wrong with these people? We are not THERE yet!" You see, for her dad, the journey WAS as much a part of the destination as getting there and he found joy in the smallest things along the way. He was so different than I was, but here's the truth, to him, the journey WAS the destination!

As we invest in the lives of others, we must understand this foundational truth: maturity is a journey, not some mystical destination we will arrive at. When we work from this starting point, we see people through healthy lenses and we don't treat them as projects, we treat them as friends and sons and daughters. In this discussion of the journey to maturity, let's answer two questions:

- *What are the marks of a healthy, mature follower of Jesus?*

- *What paths must we help others navigate so that they become who Jesus desires them to become?*

JESUS'S GOAL FOR OUR SPIRITUAL MATURITY

There are so many things we might list as the overall goals that Jesus has for our lives, but again, let's keep it simple. Before we proceed further, let's review what was discussed in the last chapter, The Big Win. A mature son or daughter of the Lord is one who has said YES to Jesus and that YES is ever growing and expanding. Then, we shared some ideas from the life of Jesus of what Christlikeness would look like. In this chapter, let's go a bit further and simply look at the same things we've discussed from another point of view. Three guiding words typify the five traits we discussed in the last chapter; they simply "put some skin" on them. Let's dive in.

1. Nearness: Jesus lived close to the Father. Nearness WAS His life and character! We discussed this earlier in describing His life of secret devotion. In our becoming like Him, cultivating a life of nearness to the Father is everything. When people were around Jesus, they were most certainly near the Father. He devoted His life to being near Him. He allowed nothing to interfere with His deep connection to His Father God. Again, this is one of the practical goals for our mentoring and fathering of others. We don't need to teach them everything, we simply need to help them cultivate a life of nearness to the Lord. It is the root of the tree from which everything else grows. This should be one of our clear goals in helping others grow. It is a sign of maturity.

Geoffrey was a young man that entered our lives during our pastoral years. Of all the traits he took on, this one dominated his life. He began to carve out a life built around being near the

Lord. Prayer, reading, and devotion, both in secret and in small groups, became the very source of his life. As Geoffrey drew near, God kept His promise, "I will draw near to you" (James 4:8). Geoffrey's life was formed by the principle of nearness, and he became a magnate who influenced many others. His ability to sit before the Lord, labor, or simply enjoy prayer and worship was inspirational for us all. What an amazing work Jesus did in and through this young man, and it all stemmed from his life of simple nearness to Jesus.

2. Wholeness: Jesus was the most whole human being who ever walked the earth. He was whole in the way He dealt with others; He was whole in the way He looked at money and possessions; He was whole in His soul when others mistreated or rejected Him; He was whole in the way He felt about Himself; and perhaps His greatest sign of wholeness was His asking for the forgiveness of those who nailed Him to the tree as He hung there. Our King was and is the ultimate picture of absolute wholeness. The word salvation or saved, sozo in the Greek, means "to be made whole"—whole in every area of life. To be saved is to be made whole! To be like Christ is to be made utterly whole! Listen to Hebrews 7:25 (ESV), "Consequently, he is able to save to the uttermost those who draw near to God through him." This would include freedom from sin, the past, and worldly values, and a constant transformation of our life so that we become increasingly more like Jesus every day. It would include healing from wounds and hurts from our lives. It would include utter transformation—wholeness. Notice from the text above three things: A) He is able. Able to do what? B) Save to the uttermost! He is able to completely lock, stock, and barrel make us whole. He is able. He is able to not leave one area broken, wounded, bound, or missing. He is able! C) Those who draw near to God through Him. Notice the connection between wholeness and nearness in the text. Wholeness flows from nearness!

In our lives as spiritual parents, we cannot emphasize enough the need for wholeness in the lives of the people He brings our way. People will waltz into our lives with deep needs, broken places, bondages from the past, and values held by the spirit of this world; we must help them find freedom, deliverance, and restoration. We cannot help young followers of Jesus mature without finding wholeness. It is what He died to provide. It is the essence of salvation and it must be constantly upon our minds, hearts, and lips in prayer for those we father and mother!

Maria was a young woman that entered our lives via a very broken and worldly past. Earlier in her life, she had lived near the Lord, but as she grew older, the draw of this world called her name and she answered the call. When she danced into our lives, she danced with a terrible limp. She was a broken, hurt young woman filled with the guilt and shame of her decisions and lifestyle she had lived. I'll never forget when the healing began. One evening, we were all worshiping and we felt the Lord simply say, "Tell her she's forgiven!" Nothing profound, just "She's forgiven." As the words fell from our lips, she began to weep, then smile, then laugh, then dance. Maria went on to find great wholeness and began to serve the Lord with all of her heart. She answered heaven's call with great passion as she journeyed into the reality of wholeness in Jesus.

3. Usefulness: Jesus was perfectly useful in the Father's hands to serve the call of the Kingdom and the needs of people around Him. To be like Christ is to be utterly useful to the Father. The last practical thing we must help people grow in is their usefulness to the Father and to others. That would include many things: full surrender, discovering gifts, talents, and abilities that could be used serving.

These three words have been guides to us for many years. Study the diagram below and then let's talk about the various paths people are on in their journey to maturity.

DIFFERENT PATHS OF DISCIPLESHIP

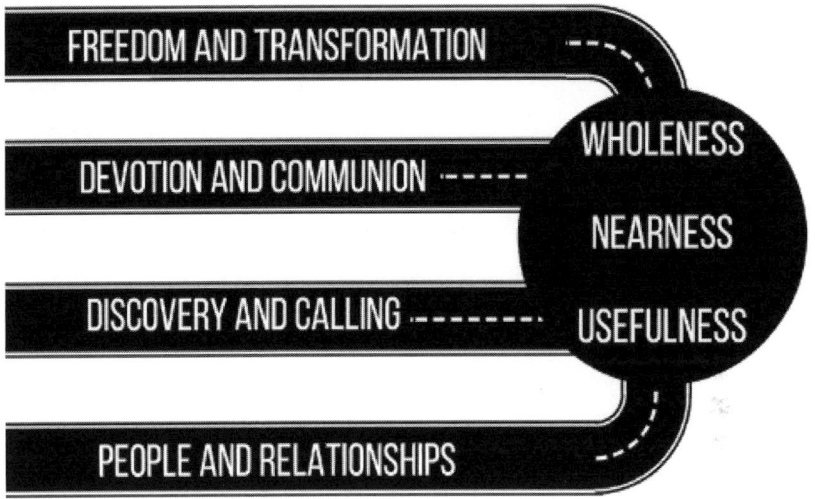

FREEDOM AND TRANSFORMATION

DEVOTION AND COMMUNION

DISCOVERY AND CALLING

PEOPLE AND RELATIONSHIPS

WHOLENESS

NEARNESS

USEFULNESS

THE MATURITY JOURNEY'S PATHS

As we seek to disciple, mentor, and father/mother others, we must understand that there is not just one path we must lead them down, but several. Every person the Father brings into our lives will be journeying down each of these paths at different increments and at different levels. To only focus on one path or one area is to be ineffective and imbalanced. In addition, the journey is different for every person because of their personality, their past, and their life situation.

As Callie and I raised our children, they were never just growing in one area at a time. They were developing intellectually, spiritually, emotionally, physically, and socially all at the same time. Wow, what a challenge to be a part of each of those paths in the lives of our children all at once. The freeing thing was, we realized that we didn't have to be the guru or doctor or specialist in any of them, we simply had to be a guide and a help along the way. I didn't teach our children calculus or volleyball, their coaches and teachers did, but it was our responsibility to see what path they needed help on and get them into the position for the right person to invest. Spiritual parenting is a team effort, much like the statement, "It takes a village to raise a child!"

Let's look at the different paths I've laid out here briefly. Each path reflects a "walk" down a set of activities, understandings, events, and growth areas the believers must go on.

The Path of Devotion: First and foremost, we must lead people down the path of personal devotion to Jesus. We chatted briefly about this in the last chapter—the life of learning to personally meet with Christ and allow Him to form, change, and shape our lives. In this path are devotions such as prayer, worship, fasting, listening, solitude, and the Bible. But also on this path are many other ways different people with different personalities draw near to the Lord. The goal of this path is ever increasing nearness to the Lord.

The Path of Freedom and Transformation: This is the path which addresses the wholeness arena of people's lives. Every person who comes to Christ comes with issues—issues of bondage, woundedness from the past, and character problems. We must learn to lead people down the path of healing, deliverance, and transformation. This path might include freedom ministry, deliverance, inner healing, or simply character and values formation. It is a critical path and we need to pay close attention to this area of people's lives. Many of us don't feel qualified to help here and might have to point others to healthy wholeness ministries around us to accomplish what the Lord desires in this area.

The Path of People: The Kingdom of God is social, and Jesus was a very social person. We are called to live and work with people. Over the years, I have seen many who are great with Jesus, but bad with people. This cannot be! We must help people down the path of people. I'll never forget when Jaxon came into my life. I was pastoring at the time and had a group of young men that met often about his age. Jaxon loved Jesus so much, but was so socially challenged that when he joined our little group, our entire group dynamics went into shock. I don't know how many times I would pull him aside and say things like, "You can't say . . . ; Jaxon, did you notice how the guys felt when you . . . ; Jaxon, you have to talk less and learn to really listen if you want people to accept you." He truly had a heart for the Lord and a call of Jesus upon his life, but Jaxon had some personality traits which caused him to not be very good with people. However, it's wonderful to watch him now. He serves the Lord in leadership of a ministry and God has done wonders. Thank God that Jaxon grew as we walked down the path of people and relationships together, because here is the truth, you will only be as useful to the Lord as you are good with people. Jesus was a master at being with and connecting with people, and it's a critical path of growth all are on. Let's help them down that path.

The Door of Surrender: This is a critical doorway and path. It's the door of us saying our YES! In every person's journey in becoming a mature son of God, they must enter the doorway of surrender to God and His will and then choose to begin walking down the path of surrender daily. Jesus said it like this, "If anyone would come after me, let him deny himself and take up his cross and follow me" (Mark 8:34 ESV). Surrender is the saying of YES to Jesus and no to that which is outside of His plan or will. It begins with a once for all decision we make before Him (by the power of His grace and grace alone!), and then it continues being worked out daily in the decisions and details of life. We must lead people to the door, and then down the pathway of surrender through our love and relationship with them. When a person surrenders to Jesus Christ, their usefulness to Him and others begins to grow. But there is a second surrender I want to share. The second surrender must follow the first. I'll tell you the story of how I first heard of the second side of surrender.

I was leading a team in Israel a few years ago and our spiritual parents, Jack and Friede Taylor, were with us. Toward the end of the trip, it appears that Jack either broke or severely injured his foot and had to stay behind as we ventured out. I was so concerned to leave him behind, but he had such joy and peace as he laid there with his swollen foot up on a pillow. I asked him, "How do you do it? How does nothing really ever get to you?" He replied, "It's the Kingdom of God. Jesus really does rule over all things concerning me and I can have peace. It's the Kingdom!" I was perplexed because I knew this cognitively in my head, but I was so far from experiencing it, so I asked, "How can I find that too, Jack?" "It's the second surrender. Many years ago, I surrendered to follow and obey, but I eventually surrendered all—everything else concerning my life into His loving hands and care! I don't have to control or worry any longer. He has it all. It's the second side of surrender!" Wow. It was like a doctoral level Bible degree from heaven's university as I sat there. Surrender is the key!

Through the doorway of initial surrender and then walking down this pathway, we lead others into a life of freedom to be in His hand that they can be useful to Him. There is little or no usefulness without the doorway and walk of surrender.

The Path of Discovery and Calling: The last pathway that disciples of Jesus must find their way down is the pathway of discovery and calling. This really only occurs after they have begun the journey of surrender. After surrendering, spiritual sons and daughters will begin to discover the gifts and abilities God is imparting to them. They will discover the more specific areas of service that God has designed for them. They will discover how to receive His anointing and empowerment for those things He is calling them to. And, ultimately, they will discover their lives bearing much fruit to the Lord. This is a path we must help them find their way down.

APPLICATION:

Think of three different people in your life whom you might disciple or mentor who are in different stages of their journey with the Lord. How might you lead each one down these paths? How would their journeys be different? Why would the journey be so different for each one? Which path is the most important at this time for each person? List specific things you might do for each to help them in their growth.

CHAPTER THIRTEEN

THE TOOLS OF THE TRADE

When Callie and I were nearing marriage, I went to work for Joe. Joe owned a construction company and out of mercy toward me and he and Terri's love for Callie, Joe hired me. At first, I just wanted to earn a few dollars, but over time, I really wanted to learn the trade and many of the necessary skills to build houses. I had no experience in any type of construction and no idea how to build a home. I had no clue about most of the tools involved. What would be the quickest way for me to learn? By working for or becoming the apprentice of a master builder! Joe and many others along the way became my teachers. Through these mentors, I discovered the basics of many of the building trades and the processes necessary to build, but their greatest gift to me was tools. They showed me <u>what tools to use</u> for each job and <u>how to use them</u> to accomplish sometimes simple and often highly complicated work. I'm grateful today for these men in my life and have since those days built several houses and remodeled many others. It's been a fun journey into the world of building and tools.

In this adventure of becoming spiritual fathers and mothers, let's turn to the master craftsman of spiritual sons—Jesus. He knows every process, every procedure, and the tools of the trade to get the job done. He spent vast amounts of His time in this exciting work of making disciples and spiritual fathering. In fact, this was second only to His revealing the Kingdom and His redemptive work of the Cross. Perhaps this is even how He revealed the Kingdom best!

When studying Jesus's life, it becomes apparent that He had many tools which He employed while investing in the men and women who followed Him. Every tool had a unique purpose in fashioning and forming each follower to have special abilities, insights, motives, and priorities. If we are to become like Him, why not pick up and learn to use the same tools that Jesus used in making His first Twelve?

JESUS'S TOOLS OF THE TRADE

The Tool of Prayer: Prayer was the first and greatest tool Jesus used to shape the lives of the men around Him. Hudson Taylor, father of the China Inland Mission, said, "I move men by prayer alone!" He picked up the tool of His Master. To simply read the Gospels just to glimpse the prayer life of Jesus is a worthy endeavor in itself, for it is full to the brim with story after story of His prayer trek through life. How did Jesus use this tool to develop His early followers?

He first prayed about his disciples, "In these days he went out to the mountain to pray, and all night he continued in prayer to God. And when day came, he called his disciples and chose from them twelve, whom he named apostles: Simon, whom he named Peter, and Andrew his brother, and James and John, and Philip, and Bartholomew, and Matthew, and Thomas, and James the son of Alphaeus, and Simon who was called the Zealot, and Judas the son of James, and Judas Iscariot, who became a traitor" (Luke 6:12–16 ESV). Already by this time in Jesus's life, He had a considerable number following, far more than the Twelve. He was about to begin a deeper investment and draw near to a few that would be His closest companions and those whom He would give His all to. How did He discover who they would be? He spent the night on a mountain asking His Father which of His followers were to be in that most intimate group.

Jesus's life was filled with prayer and we often see Him praying <u>for</u> His disciples (John 17; Luke 22:31–32). Jesus formed and fashioned His men by the power of the Holy Spirit. He received this power through time spent in prayer. Jesus prayed His disciples into becoming lovers and followers who would be full of faith and absolutely loyal to Him and to His kingdom mission. He shaped men by prayer. I'm wondering if we prayed more and said less, might we have more fruit in our lives? I'm wondering if we picked up this tool and used it fervently, what God might do in the lives and through the lives of our father and mother? He used the tool of prayer FOR them.

Third, Jesus prayed <u>with </u>His disciples (Luke 9:18; 11:1). This is one of the greatest tools in developing others. When we pray with those God has given us to father and mother, our heart and passion is revealed, our faith is exposed, our desire and motives come out, and there is a great transfer from one heart to another. Years ago, I was fathering a man named Terry. He was in a group with other men in our church leadership that I met with weekly. We studied the Bible, we prayed, we listened to each other, and we shared wisdom for life's journey. After a year, Terry pulled me aside and shared how his life had been deeply touched by our time together. I was convinced it was my always deep Bible studies, but Terry helped me see a bit clearer. Every Sunday before our weekly service, Terry, myself, and a few others would gather for an hour of prayer. Terry pointed to that hour and how every time I prayed, something of Jesus would reach out from me and touch his heart. He said, "When we prayed together, I saw into your heart and wanted a heart just like yours." Jesus invested into the lives of His men through the tool of praying WITH them. Don't we all know this? Yes, it's so simple. Most of the deeper truths of the Kingdom of God are simple. Yes, simple. Just not easy! In this business of building others, there is so much more caught than taught, and prayer is one of the greatest tools Jesus used.

The Tool of Teaching: The second great tool Jesus used in molding passionate followers and co-laborers was teaching. As we study the life of Jesus, it is easy to see that He was completely consumed with God's word, and He was completely committed to transferring the word to His disciples in many ways. Jesus Christ was a man of the word.

Jesus taught His men in many ways. He taught them formally, He explained parables to them after the formal teaching was over, and He taught them while walking along the road, while eating, or when they were arguing, etc. Jesus was always teaching. He never missed an opportunity to teach and bring them the Father's words. Look at what Jesus says is one of the signs of being a mature follower, "If you continue in My word, [then] you are truly My disciples. Then you will know the truth, and the truth will set you free" (John 8:31–32 BSB).

At the end of His life, Jesus was able to say to His Father, "For the words which You gave Me I have given to them; and they received [them] and truly understood" (John 17:8 NASB). In this statement about Jesus's own life of using the tool of teaching, we find a freeing truth—we only have to give the words He has given us! We don't have to teach them the whole Bible, the deep things of God, and the great mysteries of the Kingdom of God. We are simply responsible to be constant learners and to give the words He gives to us to those He places in our lives.

Most of us don't really feel adequate using this tool because we are not great Bible scholars or public orators. We often feel ill-equipped to "teach" others, but we underestimate all that that word could mean. Teaching can simply mean a mother sharing a life experience with another. It can mean listening to the challenge one is going through and pulling from life, giving an example of a similar circumstance and how you made it through. It could mean a planned lesson or a spontaneous response. Teaching is the art of imparting knowledge at the appropriate moment to help someone grow. I'm convinced we all can learn to use the tool of teaching but in our own unique and personal way.

When our children were young, Geoffrey, a young man in our lives, used to come to our house and had more meals at our table than a mathematician could count! He was in discipleship groups I led and was a true spiritual son. We were always "teaching" him and many others. Once while sharing with Callie and me, Geoffrey helped us understand the tool of teaching more clearly as he said, "The thing that I remember learning the most from was at meals together. How you laughed with your kids and then corrected them gently when they stepped over the line. At times, Randy would take a wayward child to the back room and they would come out loving each other, but I knew what had happened back there. Mealtimes together were the best lessons!" Teaching—we can all use the tool.

The Tool of Modeling: The third great tool Jesus used in making disciples was the tool of modeling. He learned this from His father on earth, Joseph. Joseph was a builder, perhaps a stonemason or a carpenter, and he apprenticed Jesus in His work. Jesus watched Joseph over and over as he shaped stone with his powerful hands, and He listened as Joseph talked about each step of the process. Jesus learned by watching a master at work.

Jesus trained His disciples in the same way. He showed them how to live, love, and work together with the Father. Many of the questions they asked along the way were as they watched Him pray, use His faith for some miracle, or show great compassion to a broken mother or hurting father. He was their model, and Jesus knew this was a tool of the trade. The disciples probably learned as much by watching Jesus than by what He said. People learn more from what they see in us than what they hear from us. We cannot raise people to the level of what we can teach them orally, but we can raise them to the level of what they see us working out every day in our lives.

Just as our natural children watch us and eventually become what they see in us, so do our spiritual children. <u>We cannot fake it!</u> Although our teaching is critical, our lives are even more important in the process of bringing up mature sons and daughters in the Lord. We teach with our lives. In order for this kind of teaching to really occur, Jesus had to spend much time with His disciples. Every area of His life was open before them. They didn't just see Him when He had His "ministry button" turned on, they SAW Jesus. They were constantly with Him. Many of us will allow people to be with us when we have our spiritual guard up and our "ministry switch" turned on, but they never see how we are and who we are behind the scenes. They never see US. This cannot be if we are to become healthy spiritual fathers and mothers. We must let them in! We must open our lives in full to those God has given us, and model life and ministry with Christ openly and honestly.

The Tool of Friendship: Perhaps the most powerful tool in Jesus's bag was the tool of friendship. He became the closest companion to those who chose to follow Him. Jesus changed lives through being with His disciples. Look at what the Scripture says about Jesus, "And he appointed twelve . . . that they might be with him" (Mark 3:14 ESV).

Jesus chose 12 men and then gave them an assignment: <u>to be with Him.</u> They would learn through sharing life together, laughing, working, loving, and living together—they would become friends. And through the power of this purpose-filled friendship, Jesus planned to change the world! Toward the end of their time together, Jesus said, "You are My friends, if you do what I command you. No longer do I call you servants, for the servant does not know what his master is doing. But I have called you friends, because all things that I heard from My father, I have made known to you. You did not choose Me, but I chose you and appointed you, that you should go and bear fruit" (John 15:14–16 BSB).

This was not just a casual friendship. In the mind of Jesus, it was a focused friendship with one purpose—to give His disciples everything that He had received from the Father. He knew that a classroom could not do it. It would take living life together, and only friendship would open that possibility.

As disciples of Jesus ourselves, when we disciple others as moms and dads, we cannot limit our friendship to a classroom or a sermon. We must give our sons and daughters our time and our lives. Just as Jesus lived life with His men, so must we. Paul said of the Thessalonians, "Having thus a fond affection for you, we were well-pleased to impart to you not only the gospel of God but also our own lives, because you had become very dear to us" (1 Thessalonians 2:8 NAS 1977).

The Tool of Practical Ministry Assignments: Jesus changed their lives and helped them grow up by putting them to work with Him and for Him. While with His Twelve, Jesus constantly gave them practical ministry assignments. He knew that to be a mature follower, didn't mean just learning lessons from Him. It also meant joining Him in His life work amongst the broken of the world. Jesus discipled through putting them to work, hard work.

He didn't limit His maturing touch on their lives to simply their heads and hearts; He also ministered to their hands and feet. He brought the gospel and life He was preaching down into simple reality and good works. Here are some of the things Jesus gave His disciples to do:

- *He had them feed 5,000 people.*

- *He sent them to preach.*

- *He had them heal people and cast out demons.*

- *He had them care for the poor.*

- *They prepared rooms and meals for the group and for others.*

- *He had them pray for others.*

Please don't allow your spiritual proteges to be selfish and heady believers. Put them to work. It's through bearing responsibility that we become strong. It's through hard work that we grow. It's through practical serving that our hands train.

The Tool of Faith Challenges: One of the most important areas to help followers of Jesus to grow in is in the area of faith. Faith is that all-important ingredient in the human heart, which will cause a man to fail or succeed. Without faith, we cannot please God, follow Him, or love Him. One of the great secrets of Jesus's life of discipling is that He constantly placed His men in situations which tested their faith. Would they believe Him and believe the Father, or would they doubt? Would they reach into the realm of the Spirit and get supernatural answers, or would they only react in the natural power and wisdom of their own flesh? These faith challenges were some of the most life-transforming moments in the Twelve disciples' lives.

I love the text in Jesus's life found in John 6:1–13 where He fed the 5,000 plus. In John's recording of this wonderful day, he shares that Jesus asked Philip to figure out how to feed the whole mass. Philip comes back to Jesus saying that it's impossible; it can't be done with what they have or where they are. But then Andrew steps up and offers a little boy's lunch. Jesus just smiled then produced a mighty miracle through the hands of His followers. Even Philip's unbelieving hands were a source of this great sign. In verse six, John tells us that He asked Philip the question to test him. What was the test? Could he step out of his natural thinking and believe for the miraculous? Philip failed this test but grew through the process of being placed over and over in "faith" moments.

As we disciple others, we cannot miss this all-important ingredient. When Jesus was done with His Twelve, they could live and move in the power of faith. That was one of their great secrets. In the same way, we must (under the leading of the Holy Spirit) place those whom we are discipling in circumstances and moments of faith. We should help our sons and daughters in Jesus find themselves in situations where they have no alternative but to trust God so that the genuineness of their faith might come forth. There is no other way to mature.

JESUS'S METHOD OF DISCIPLING: SPIRITUAL FATHERING

All that Jesus did with His Twelve men, and all the tools He used in discipling them, can be summarized in one term: spiritual fathering. Although Jesus was a friend to the disciples, He was also like a father to them. Jesus related to and trained the Twelve in the same way that a father relates to his natural son in order to mature him and raise him up. On the last night of Jesus's life, this conversation took place: "Philip said to Him, 'Lord, show us the Father, and it is enough for us.' Jesus said to him, 'Have I been so long with you, and [yet] you have not come to know Me, Philip? He who has seen Me has seen the Father; how can you say, "Show us the Father?'" (John 14:8–9 NASB) They were asking to see the Father, but what they didn't realize was that everything Jesus was doing with them was the Father. And how was He doing it? As a spiritual father and friend.

APPLICATION:

Break into a group of three and let each one in the group give the name of some real person in their life that might be a disciple/son candidate. Using the list of names you've given as a mock discipleship group, write out a strategy showing how you might use all six of the tools Jesus used to disciple your group of young believers. Be very clear and specific on how you might use these tools practically.

CHAPTER FOURTEEN

ATTITUDE IS EVERYTHING

As we begin to work with younger (or sometimes older followers of Jesus), we will realize that it's not just our attitude that matters, but their attitude towards Jesus and we, who will father or mother them, is absolutely critical for maturity and growth. In parenting our own children, there have been times when it was one of the most joyful experiences in our lives, but at other times, it was like slogging through mud in snowshoes. What made the difference? Attitude—our kids' attitudes.

One great writer said, "Your living is determined not so much by what life brings to you, as by the attitude you bring to life." Winston Churchill went on to say, "Attitude is a little thing that makes a big difference!" Attitude is the open door of the human heart to be taught, trained, and brought into maturity, or it is a closed door of blindness that leads to perpetually running around in circles. Those that we father or mother must have a proper attitude, that is, that the door of the heart is truly open to input from another. If not, we will only be wasting our time.

People often ask me, "Well, do I just wait until I find someone with the perfectly right attitude and then I'll dive into investing in their lives?" If that was true, Jesus would have never begun His life or ministry of making disciples. Instead, He got in the boat with them and cultivated the proper attitudes in them along the way. In saying this, I in no way think we should just jump in the boat with anyone. They have to have some fundamental hunger and openness to even begin the journey, but it's our job as spiritual parents to help them cultivate healthy attitudes, which throw the human heart wide open to growth and change. With that said, let's look into the necessary attitudes within those we will father and mother.

CRITICAL ATTITUDES FOR MAXIMUM GROWTH

The Attitude of Hunger and Availability: One of the key marks of an emerging follower of Jesus is hunger and availability. The disciples of Jesus were passionately hungry for God, and they saw that they would find more of God in their relationship with Jesus. They also left all behind—they made their practical lives very available to be with Jesus, sticking to Him like glue. Once He had said to them, "Follow Me." The responsibility was no longer on Jesus; it was on the disciple. A spiritual father makes the offer, but it is up to the disciple to follow. This is the first and perhaps most crucial attitude in the lives of our spiritual children if our investment is going to pay dividends. Without a hungry heart and without them being available to spend time in some form with us, we can't get very far.

I'll never forget a few years ago, a young man I was spending some time with asked to be filled with the Holy Spirit. As we began to pray together, he fell asleep! Yes, asleep. I stopped praying, woke him up, and told him he was wasting both of our time. He got a bit offended, but a few months later, the Lord had so worked in his heart that he asked for the Spirit infilling once again, and this time, he didn't fall asleep. He received the glorious gift of God, and his life has never been the same. That's the power of hunger, but availability is just as vital. If Bill, or Sasha, or Maria, or Thomas don't have time to meet with you, THEN THEY DON'T HAVE TIME TO MEET WITH YOU. Don't chase them, ask the Father for another. Many times in Jesus's life, He called men to follow Him only to get the response of, "I have to go and do . . . first, and then when I'm done, I'll come back and follow You." He never chased them down. He just went on His way with those who had made their lives available.

The Attitude of Servanthood: The disciples of Jesus served Him. They joined Him in the things that the Father had given Him to accomplish and attend to, but they went far beyond that; they served HIM. They loved Him, cared for His needs, and made sure that which concerned Him, concerned them. In healthy, loving families it's no different. Our kids served; they always served.

Callie is amazed when parents allow their children all the benefits of being in the family with absolutely no or little responsibility. We have friends who deeply loved their children, but who have shouldered an entire load of daily family life on their own, never asking much from their offspring. They didn't want to burden or put too much on their children so they could enjoy their lives. Wow, Callie feels this is one of the greatest disservices we can do in parenting. Life is not a vacation or party; it's a journey with both fun and hard work along the way. To not train our children in serving is to cripple them from the necessary skills needed to both be successful in life and be true followers of Jesus. How many times did Jesus speak of serving? In fact, to be the greatest in the Kingdom of God one should become the servant of all.

Shouldn't it be the same with those we disciple and father or mother? They should serve. They should serve alongside us in the work God has given us when able, but they should also have the heart to do acts of service toward us who father and mother them. This is healthy. This is true family. I've seen those in spiritual authority take this principle beyond healthy levels, controlling and demanding those "under" them to serve them; this should never be. But, serving the one who is investing in your life in the Lord IS a very clear principle in Scripture.

- *Elisha Served Elijah: After the Lord told Elijah to anoint Elisha as his successor, Elisha became Elijah's attendant. This word literally means "one who pours water." He used to pour water on the hands of Elijah.*

- *The Twelve Served Jesus: It is clear in the Scriptures that the disciples served Jesus. A rabbi's disciple was responsible for many things, including caring for the needs of his teacher and carrying out the rabbi's commands and wishes.*

- *Timothy Served Paul: "As a son with his father he has served with me in the work of the gospel" (Philippians 2:22 NIV).*

The Attitude of Imitating: In a healthy family, kids imitate their parents, and so it is in the Kingdom of God. A remarkable attitudinal trait that helps growth is to follow those who are discipling by imitating their lives in character, word, and deed. Paul appealed to the Corinthians, "Therefore I urge you to imitate me," and explained that he would help them to do that by sending Timothy to them. Paul was confident that Timothy would remind them of his "way of life in Christ Jesus," because Paul had fathered Timothy well and said, "I have no one else like him."

The root of the Greek word meaning imitate is *mimos* which gives us the English word "mimic". Imitating is also taught in other passages, where the same Greek word is sometimes translated "follow my example":

- *"Follow my example, as I follow the example of Christ" (1 Corinthians 11:1 NIV).*

- *"You became imitators of us and of the Lord" (1 Thessalonians 1:6 NIV).*

- *"Remember your leaders, who spoke the word of God to you. Consider the outcome of their way of life and imitate their faith" (Hebrews 13:7 NIV).*

The Attitude of Honor: "'Honor your father and mother'—which is the first commandment with a promise—so that it may go well with you and that you may enjoy long life on the earth'" (Ephesians 6:1–3 NIV). The Bible instructs us to honor our father and mother. This applies to the spiritual realm as well as the natural; such honoring does not restrict us, but opens the way for God's blessing.

It's amazing that the very Son of God had the most difficulty at times not because of harsh persecution, but because of a lack of honor. Once in His own hometown as He taught and began to administer the Spirit in healing, the miracles shut off. Why? Dishonor. Listen to the text, "He went away from there and came to his hometown . . . And on the Sabbath he began to teach in the synagogue, and many who heard him were astonished, saying, 'Where did this man get these things? What is the wisdom given to him? How are such mighty works done by his hands? Is not this the carpenter, the son of Mary and brother of James and Joses and Judas and Simon? And are not his sisters here with us?' And they took offense at him. And Jesus said to them, 'A prophet is not without honor, except in his hometown and among his relatives and in his own household.' And he could do no mighty work there, except that he laid his hands on a few sick people and healed them. And he marveled because of their unbelief" (Mark 6:1–6 ESV). How did this dishonoring of Jesus unfold? As they heard Him and saw God work through Him, they stumbled over his humanity. Why? He had grown up there. He was the son of the carpenter. He was Mary's boy who had never done anything special in the village before. Something was wrong here. They stumbled over Jesus's humanity, even though it was sinless humanity!

If not careful, those we mentor will fall into the same trap of dishonoring us, whom God has sent to help mature them and help them grow up. The closer one gets to another, or the closer we let someone into our lives, the more we/they will see imperfect humanity and the greater the temptation to reject the gift because of character issues or human quirkiness. I'm not saying we should follow people with terrible character or deep sin, but I am saying that all humans are human. We are human and will have flaws, sins, and broken places in our lives. We cannot let that hinder us from giving or receiving from another, and we must teach those who follow us this principle of honoring their father and mother.

Here are some ways a son or daughter can show honor to their spiritual parents:

- *By expressing affection with words and other forms of appropriate affection, as well as celebrating birthdays, wedding anniversaries, and special events.*

- *By respecting your spiritual parents. That is, you consider them above yourself, think highly of them, and want them to be praised. You are not frightened of them; rather, you look up to them with a healthy respect.*

- *By being loyal to them. Even if your spiritual father or mother falls into sin or hard times, you will stick close to them and honor them, helping them overcome. At times, we will all have to overlook and be forbearing with one another. We are different. We have broken places in our lives and will make mistakes. Honor treats one another with great grace.*

- *By listening attentively to what they say—both instructions and opinions. Try to pick up what is on their heart, and see if there is something you should be implementing.*

Attitude is crucial, critical, and very important. As we were raising our natural-born children, we not only disciplined and spoke into their behaviors, we went deeper; we cultivated their attitudes, and at times even brought loving discipline there, for the saying is so true, "Your attitude determines your altitude!"

THE BEGINNINGS

In the beginning of my life of discipling others, I was a methodologist—I wanted a clear program, a very pragmatic method. "For the sake of the Kingdom, someone just tell me exactly what to teach them and exactly how to do it, step by step, please. And by the way, make sure one size fits all because Jesus never changes!" The problem is pretty clear though—

everyone is different, they all are at different places in their lives, going through different things, and <u>one size never fits all</u>. To be honest, everyone I tried to disciple or father in those early days was a "project"—I knew it and unfortunately, they did too. It's just not fun being treated like a project.

Over the years, Callie, myself, and our great friend and coworker at PI, Drew Brown, spent thousands of hours collectively discipling, mentoring, fathering and mothering 100s, and I have good news for you . . . I learned to treat people like people. Whew! That's a big win for all of us. What follows in this chapter is a way of thinking that emerged in all three of us, and as we put our heads together years ago, we put words and a bit of practical methodology to what we had learned so we could pass it on to others. We have shared this approach to fathering all over the world, and when we do, the lights come on. People have said over and over, "Wow, I can do this! It's natural, and yet it's a clear approach to investing in others with clear paths and desired outcomes at the end."

We are using "cups" to illustrate this model because of the imagery involved, and to be very honest a good portion of our time with disciples is spent with a cup of coffee in hand. Each of the Five Cups represents an essential life category that we want to help others to grow in. Over the years, after working with 100s and perhaps 1000s, we discovered that all of life falls into one of five big categories/cups. Fathering and mothering, with the help of the Holy Spirit, is the process of filling each cup in a person's life, creating a mature Kingdom life.

UNDERLYING PRINCIPLES TO GUIDE US

Everyone Is Different: This is obvious to most of you reading this booklet, but it wasn't with me. I just wanted a method and program I could impose on people in Jesus's name. But the problem is clear—everyone is different and needs a different ingredient for growth at that specific moment. What Tom needs today to grow is probably not what Sam needs, and vice versa.

This method begins from the place that everyone is different and needs similar ingredients, but not at the same time and often not in the same measure. Another idea we've discovered is that what is important to a person's growth today may not be what they need two weeks from now. This method not only takes into account the differences between people, but it also allows that each time you or I meet with someone, their personal need at that moment may also be different.

Join God in Where He Is Working: I normally meet with people over a cup of coffee. I really believe everything is better and everything is somehow "right" in the world with a good, steaming cup in hand. Somehow it causes me to go "shoooooooosh" and slow everything down to a crawl. The pace of crawl is so needed to really see what a person needs and what God is doing at that moment. As I get near the place of meeting, I often pray, "Holy Spirit, I have no idea what You are doing and what Sam needs from You or me. I ask You to work powerfully in our short time together and lead me through Sam's own sharing to where you are working."

Ask Questions and Then Respond to Where He Is Working: When we get together, I simply start asking questions about things in daily life: "What's the Lord been putting on your heart lately? How's your family? What's going on with . . .? What's the biggest struggle you've been dealing with lately?" I might also ask a question about something we had previously spoken or prayed together about. All of these questions circle around the five big categories or cups of life we will look at in just a moment. And through asking and listening, I simply trust that the Spirit will lead Sam to which of the cups is most important for that moment in life. Perhaps, he might "park his car" and talk for 20 minutes about a situation with his wife or with a child. Or perhaps, he might begin to talk about big character issues he sees in himself and the world around him. Here's the principle: wherever Sam parks his car and talks as you listen, is probably where the Lord is working and that's where you should work too.

Christ the Center: A fourth principle we use to guide us is: everything flows out of our life with Jesus at the center. If you pictured five cups on a table with one in the center and the other four surrounding it, that center cup is our relationship to God through Jesus Christ; it's our faith life. When that one is growing and being filled, it tends to overflow, and both fix and fill the others. I always try to keep Christ at the center as I disciple and encourage others.

Once we land on a topic, I listen for a while and then begin to share. It might be a verse of Scripture or simply a story of something I went through years back, but I park my car of sharing at the same cup Sam does and simply try to add one thing in that area that will help him grow, mature, and be victorious in that area. Keep it simple as you share; they don't need an exegesis on the book of Deuteronomy; they just need truth in the place that God is at work. Someone great once said, "the truth will set you free." Now, let's look at the foundation stone of this whole approach: the Five Cups.

CHAPTER FIFTEEN

THE FIVE CUPS

1. THE FAITH CUP

The beginning of all things in the Kingdom of God is your faith life with Jesus. To help anyone grow and become mature, without making this the center of all, is to deceive yourself and those you mentor. Our intimacy, faith, love, hope, and life in Jesus is the central cup on the table of life, and as I share life with others, I point them here all the time. How can we measure our or another's relationship with God? Simple, the fruit of Jesus in our lives. We can keep our eyes on someone's pursuit of God and are they responding to Him. We need to encourage people to spend priority time with God in devotion and prayer, in listening for His voice and obeying His word. This is the faith area of life.

As you father or mother, simply share your own experiences (successes and failures) in your life with Jesus. Practical things like:

- *How often do you read and study the Bible? How did you make it a habit? How do you deal with days where you don't get anything out of what you are reading? What resources do you use to help you understand scriptures when the meaning is unclear?*

- *Share how you cultivated a time set aside to talk to God and listen to His voice. How did you face the struggle of feeling like you couldn't hear Him? Share times you experienced a breakthrough in hearing the Holy Spirit.*

- *Share how you nurtured worship in your life. What seems to draw you into God's presence?*

- *Share how you made decisions and took steps of bold faith at times and leaned into wisdom at others. Have you made any big decisions that required you to act on faith? What happened? How have you grown in your trust in God's way? How have you learned to trust God with every part of your life?*

No matter what cup the Lord leads us to discuss in that gettogether, I always try to make one small deposit in a person's heart and life of faith. It might just be praying together at the end, or perhaps we are discussing marriage, and I'll share about the absolute necessity of Jesus being Lord of all for a healthy marriage or else selfishness rules. The other four cups can only be filled if the faith cup is overflowing! Put one thing into Christ being the center every chance you get, but don't stop there.

2. THE RELATIONSHIP CUP

Our maturity can often be measured by our relationships (or the absence of them). God desires for us to have healthy, life-giving relationships, and He has given us all the opportunity to learn how to engage in a godly, Spirit-filled way. As you father and mother, the second big cup is the cup of relationships. Only as we discover and enter into a healthy, growing, life-giving relationship can we be whole and useful to God and His world.

I used to be terrible at relationships and thought that Jesus and I are enough. It sounds spiritual, but only if you're called to live in a cave somewhere out of life's real reach. It's been a long road learning to relate, to listen, to care, and above all, to connect with others on a heart level. To be honest, I'm still a bit broken and undeveloped in this area. Callie, on the other hand, is a master of relating and connecting. When she connects, she connects. She's a great listener, a great carer, a wonderful relater, and I've learned so much from her. Only as we grow and relate are we truly whole or of service to this world.

As you work with others, never underestimate the importance of the health of the relationships in their lives. Focus on things like:

- *Do you understand what it takes to be a good friend? Are you experiencing good friendships? How are you dealing with family relationships? What about romantic relationships? If you are married, how are you building a strong marriage?*

- *In your relationships, is your natural tendency to give, or do you struggle with always taking? How has the Holy Spirit helped you lie down inappropriate expectations in your relationships?*

- *When you experience disagreements, is your priority to win the argument or to build the relationship? Has the Holy Spirit helped you learn to lovingly bring confrontation when needed, or do you still avoid confrontation at all costs?*

- *Have you learned to forgive and truly forget? Have you learned to be patient and accepting of others when they are different from you? Have you learned to celebrate and appreciate those differences?*

- *Have you learned to listen as much or more than you talk? Have you learned to shut off outside noise and distractions when you are with those you love?*

Healthy relationships lead to healthy community life and healthy families. Followers of Jesus must continually seek to express the fruit of the Spirit in all relationships.

3. THE CHARACTER CUP

Character is the sum of our attitudes, inner thought life, and our tendency toward action or inaction. It reveals such things as whether you are trustworthy, honest, and willing to work hard. Jesus's teaching in Matthew 5–7 largely encourages us to take on His own character. One of my early mentors often said, "the Kingdom of God is Christlikeness." If that is true, then our character is critical.

Sharing your experience and struggles are always a good way to discuss the area of character with those you are discipling. Have you struggled with finishing things you start? Have you failed to keep promises? Have you been tempted to only do the minimum work required, instead of giving your best all of the time? When did you learn to truly forgive someone that hurt you? How have you learned to lie down offenses? How did you learn to live in purity and integrity?

These are issues of character, and it is important to help spiritual children pursue the character of Jesus that we see in Matthew 5–7. Of course, all character growth comes as a result of the Holy Spirit's work and the production of the Spirit's fruit (Galatians 5:22), so it is always essential to nurture the ability to hear and obey the Spirit's voice.

Most people become overly concerned with what others THINK about them. But, our self-awareness should focus more on WHAT JESUS thinks of us and how our presence AFFECTS OTHERS. Matthew 5 reveals Jesus's goal for our character when He reveals His own character. The first 10 verses are character traits that tune our lives into the character of Jesus. Jesus recognizes His utter need of the Father (poor in spirit); He also quickly enters into the heartache of others (blessed are those that mourn); He is quick to offer mercy and bring peace (merciful and peacemakers).

REFLECTION:

How much of our behavior is not a reflection of who we are, but a reflection of what we want others to see? What effect do you have on others when they are in your presence? Do they receive something of God?

APPLICATION:

In preparation to share with others in the area of character, spend a few minutes writing down some details of your own journey in character growth. See if you can identify some key turning points where you saw big changes in your maturity along the way. What have you learned from the Holy Spirit that could encourage others as they face their own character issues?

4. THE FINANCE CUP

Money is a direct window into our hearts. Jesus says it well, "for where your treasure is, there will your heart be also" (Matthew 6:21 KJB). Money is the third most discussed subject by Jesus in the New Testament. How we make, spend, give, and/or save our money reveals much about our relationship with God. Learning to allow God to have control of our money is a key step in our growth as a disciple of Jesus.

There have been so many scandals of famous "men of God" who mishandled money and brought disgrace to Jesus and the Body of Christ. On top of that, how can we be a praise to God on the earth that the lost in our world see if our monetary and possession life is completely out of order? Money, possessions, and work are not necessary evils but are natural demonstrators of our life in Jesus. Money matters!

As we work with others to help them grow and mature in Jesus Christ, let's not neglect their financial life. Jesus didn't! Here are some questions and thoughts to guide:

- *What is Jesus's attitude about money? What is yours?*

- *What does the Apostle Paul teach us about money? (2 Corinthians 9:6–11) What should be our view of money?*

- Do you truly believe that God, not money, is your source?

- Have you learned to work hard and give your best on the job daily?

- What has God taught you about tithing? What are your financial goals? What are your giving goals?

- Do you know where your money is going? How much do you spend on entertainment compared to food or utilities? Have you taken the time to create a budget? Do you struggle with staying within your budget?

- Do you have a good balance between a blessed and excellent life and simplicity with generosity?

- Do you struggle with the love of money or the fear of lack?

As you sit with others and listen, open your eyes and listen well for this area. It cannot be overlooked. Be ready to share both financial struggles and moments of breakthrough in your own financial life. Don't be afraid to call them into the kingship of Jesus in the financial area of life.

5. THE MINISTRY CUP

Ministry should flow from a healthy life in the other four cups. I've met many who are not growing and being victorious either spiritually or in practical daily life, yet they are chasing a "call" from God. Let's disciple the whole man; we cannot neglect a person's giving of their lives for Jesus with others. This is the life of ministry.

We must encourage those we father and mother to give their lives to Jesus for the sake of the world. I'll never forget when our natural kids were young how we annually took them to a world mission conference to stir the fires of ministry in their young hearts. Once, the Saturday evening speaker shared relentless stories of his own life going to some of the most difficult, unreached parts of the earth. Wow, a lost man would have committed his life to serving Jesus that night. At the end, all of our kids stood at his altar call, to go to the hard places of the earth. We were shocked, a bit scared, and yet proud. The heart for the world and service to both God and man was being cultivated in their blossoming lives. This is what moms and dads do. They develop Kingdom-life purpose in their children, and this is what we call ministry.

Focus on things like:

- *Cultivating a life of general service and doing good to all around. This is the beginning place of all ministry. It doesn't begin with a calling from God, it begins with Jesus's simple calling to serve others. Have you dedicated your time and efforts to serving others? If you've experienced sacrificial service, what was it like? How were you able to do it?*

- *What do you feel God has called you to do? Based on Romans 12:6–8, what areas of gifting might you have? Are there any areas of gifting that make you excited to think about? Have you experienced God using you to minister to others? What was it like?*

- *What kinds of things can you do to grow in your ability to serve others?*

- *When are people most blessed by your service, and how do you feel when you do that thing?*

Encourage them like crazy to give their lives away and share stories about your own life and how you learned to serve. Share how you began to discover your gifts and how you use them. Help them discover a life of laying down their lives and blessing the world around them.

SMALL GROUP DISCUSSION:

In each of the Five Cup categories:

- *Can you identify ways that you have personally grown?*

- *What are two questions that you could ask to help someone assess how they are maturing?*

- *Identify two suggestions to help someone grow as a disciple.*

THE PRINCIPLE OF ONE SMALL THING

In the early days of using the Five Cup strategy for discipling, I made the mistake of trying to completely fill the cup the Lord led us to that day and the faith cup every time I met with someone. I put tremendous pressure on myself to fill that cup! Over time, I realized that the MORE I tried to put in the cup in one short coffee meeting, the LESS that really stayed in there! I don't have to teach them everything; I just need to put one small thing in where Jesus is already at work and then point them to their faith in Jesus being the center of life. Wow, the pressure came off, and I learned not to overfill the cup until everything ran out. If I will make one small addition to a cup, then they can grab it and begin to live it in daily life. This has become one of the greatest discoveries of my life—a little bit truly goes a long way when I give a little bit over and over and over in a person's life.

USING THE FIVE CUPS AS A DISCIPLESHIP MODEL

This model for discipleship answers the common question, "What am I supposed to talk about when I meet with people I am discipling?" In fact, it provides two services for those of us who want to heed the call to disciple others. First, it provides a way for us to assess our own journey as a disciple of Christ.

Understanding our own spiritual journey helps us to know what we need to focus on in our own maturity. Second, this model provides specific content for discussion and helps us see the journey of those we disciple in wholistic-life terms. As we become familiar with the five categories of life, we learn to pay attention to priority needs while keeping a balance, making sure that all areas of growth are given proper attention.

Chapter Sixteen

BABES, KIDS, AND YOUNG MEN

As we near the end of our journey together discovering life in the Father/Son Paradigm, let's chat a few minutes about one of the key ingredients of being a good spiritual father or mother—understanding your spiritual children. I've said this many times throughout this booklet, but I desperately wanted a one-size and one-method-fits-all approach to being a dad in the natural. It didn't work out too well for me and was a disaster for our children. They had different personalities, different leanings and bents; and one was a boy, and two came out as girls. That sure threw a wrench into the machinery. It seemed every time I began to get a handle on helping them grow, feel secure, and find their place, they changed; they matured. Understanding spiritual children's different stages of maturity are critical to serving as a healthy and helpful spiritual mentor and guide.

It works like this: you can't treat a two-year-old like he is 30, because he's not ready for the responsibility and has needs that a 30-year-old does not. Conversely, don't treat a 30-year-old like he is two; that would be demeaning and degrading, and your relationship wouldn't last very long. If it did, then instead of you being a stepping stone to maturity and fruitfulness, you would be a brutal stumbling block.

I thank God that John had the foresight, under the guidance of the Holy Spirit, to describe the different phases of maturity we all pass through along the road toward maturity. John makes it clear and gives us great insight into understanding different stages of maturation along the Kingdom journey.

Understanding Their Stage of Maturity

> "I am writing to you, <u>little children</u>, because your sins are forgiven for his name's sake.
>
> I am writing to you, <u>fathers</u>, because you know him who is from the beginning.
>
> I am writing to you, <u>young men</u>, because you have overcome the evil one.
>
> I write to you, <u>children</u>, because you know the Father.
>
> I write to you, <u>fathers</u>, because you know him who is from the beginning.
>
> I write to you, <u>young men</u>, because you are strong, and the word of God abides in you, and you have overcome the evil one."
>
> 1 John 2:12–14 (ESV)

Little Children: *Teknion*: infant, very young baby. These are those spiritual sons and daughters who are brand new in the faith, or have come to Christ and have not grown past the beginning stages; they are like little babies who either need constant care or feel they need nothing at all. If they have been in Christ for any length of time and are still at this point, then the person has ceased to grow or function spiritually; they are spiritually stunted or perhaps even dead. God's forgiveness is the attribute these infants are primarily concerned with. Their thoughts about their new life in Jesus go something like this, "I am forgiven; I am going to heaven; I am in the Kingdom, and that is all I am concerned about." These believers can be characterized by the statement, "It is all about me." Isn't that how babies operate?

Children: *Paidion*: young boy or girl. In describing a child's physical growth, this stage goes up to about 13 years old. This level of a person's spiritual growth is characterized by the fact that they know the Father. These are people who are growing and have genuinely begun a relationship with God as their Father. Notice that this does not say <u>Master</u>. We come into the Kingdom through receiving Christ as Lord and Master, but to stay only in that relationship is <u>not</u> normal. We should add to the initial Lordship relationship and begin to know the Father and to know what it is like to be a son of God. This is the natural progression for maturity in Christ—believers begin to be set free from an orphan mentality and live as a true son. People at this level can be characterized by the statement, "It is all about the Father and me."

Young Men: *Neaniskos*: under the age of 40. This phrase denotes the age of physical growth that begins in the teenage years and lasts until a person is about 40 years old. Spiritually, the primary traits developed during this stage are deep inner strength, the Word of God abiding in the believer, and overcoming the evil one. In the society of the Apostle John's day, the young men were those in society who fought the wars, built the cities, ran the farms, and had children. These were the ones that life and productivity were built upon. Notice these three marks of the mature young man (remember ladies, this is genderless!):

- *Strong: One becomes strong through much hard work (mentally, spiritually, emotionally) and through facing and overcoming resistance of differing sorts. There is no other way.*

- *The Word of God Abides in Them: Something has happened in these lives. They no longer simply know God's word in their minds—it has now become a part of them. The Word of God resides deeply within them, guiding them, speaking to them, and giving them life.*

- *Have Overcome the Evil One: This speaks of warfare. These young men have learned to engage in warfare and have learned to win. They not only can win in their own lives, but they also have become victors for the lives of others.*

This is our goal in spiritual parenting—to produce "young men." We need both male and female young men! These are the ones who will give their lives for Christ and His work, and be effective in it. We must have young men. They are characterized by the statement, "It is all about Father and His world!"

Fathers: These are men and women who have walked with God for many years and know Him intimately. They have given their lives to Him and are committed to producing sons who will do God's will. This is who WE must become. God is looking for a new harvest, a harvest of fathers and mothers who will give their lives for the rapid and deep-maturing of the saints.

As we begin to invest ourselves in the lives of others, we should have a good idea of where they are in the progression of maturity. We don't want to stereotype people, but knowing the process and what level people are currently in will help us begin to serve, love, and invest in them effectively, right where they are.

SMALL GROUP DISCUSSION:

Identify at least one person you know in each level of spiritual growth. What would you do with each to help them continue to grow?

Little Child:

Child:

Young Man:

Father:

MINISTERING TO THE DIFFERENT STAGES

The following diagram describes the growth we want to see in those we are discipling, based upon the teaching of John using the levels of growth: Little Child, Child, Young Man, and Father.

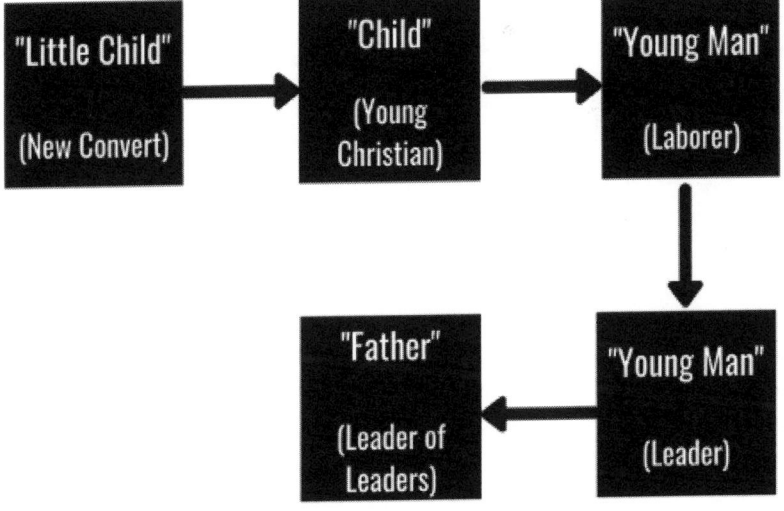

THE PRINCIPLE OF PROACTIVE/REACTIVE

An important principle to learn, as you begin to disciple people through these different stages of their Christian life, is how proactive you should be. Should you initiate all the ministry? Or should you react to what you see or hear from them? Jesus was very proactive at times, initiating ministry to the Twelve. At other times in His discipling, Jesus would react to something His followers did or said.

On top of the principle I just shared, we must understand that some people are very aggressive and proactive by nature; hence, their fathering/mothering style will look very proactive. Whereas, others are more reactive by nature; that is, they simply keep their eyes and ears open and take advantage of opportunities whenever they arise. It is important to understand how God made you and to be comfortable with yourself. However, all of us can grow to some extent on the other side of the proactive/reactive equation.

The more mature the person you are discipling is, the more reactive your ministry with them will be. On the other hand, when you are discipling an infant in Christ, you will need to be very proactive with them—just like parents of new babies have to have a good plan to care for their new little one.

LITTLE CHILDREN: MINISTERING TO BABES: THE MINISTRY OF ESTABLISHING

New converts or baby Christians are what John called "little children" or "infants" in 1 John. When a new baby is born into a family, the early care of that child is critical to its' life and development. It is the same with a newborn babe in Christ. The goal of this process is to bring the believer to the point of being established in Christ and the spiritual community. We want to produce children in the Lord who are solid followers of Jesus and consistent in their spiritual relationships.

What Do We Teach the New Babes?

How to Breathe: Prayer. Every baby needs to learn to breathe on their own. In the Kingdom, prayer is the very breath of a believer's life. From the beginning, a new convert must be taught how to simply and consistently communicate with the Father; this is prayer. As we teach the young Christian about prayer, here are some essentials:

- *How to confess sin (1 John 1:9).*

- *How to make requests based upon promises.*

- *How to listen and hear His voice.*

How to Eat: The Bible is the source of daily food for all children of God. If a baby does not eat, it will not grow; it is the same with all believers. We must teach young ones in the Lord to eat the Word of God. It isn't necessary to teach them the Word of God itself in all of its depth and complexity, so much as how to eat for themselves. We don't want to create a totally dependent baby; we want mature sons of God. Here are three practices we must teach:

- *Daily Bible reading.*

- *How to memorize Scripture.*

- *How to study and how to meditate when God begins to speak out of a passage.*

Family: The need for a loving, consistent family. All children need two kinds of family relationships: a loving father and/or mother and good brothers and sisters. We must teach the new convert about the church and their relationship to others in the body. At the same time, we must create an environment of acceptance and love required for their growth. All babies make a lot of messes when they are first born. They mess their diaper (and often everything around them), as so do baby Christians. We must be there to clean them up when they make a mess.

Different people come to us with different levels of problems in their lives, and we need to be there for them. Some will have so many problems that we don't quite know if we can help clean them up. Remember, time and consistency are on our side.

How to Exercise the New Muscles: Obedience and Faith. One of the mistakes many make when they disciple new converts is to expect too little of them at first. We must teach them to exercise their spiritual muscles immediately. Three ways we can do this include:

- *Teaching them to obey all that God shows them.*

- *Teaching them to find His promises and claim His supernatural answers.*

- *Teaching them to bring their lost friends and loved ones to the Lord.*

Often, baby Christians are the greatest evangelists we have, so we must learn to encourage them in these early days.

CHILDREN: MINISTERING TO YOUNG CHRISTIANS: THE MINISTRY OF GROUNDING IN FAITH AND SERVANTHOOD

Once we have established the babes in Christ and the Church, our next goal is to work with the Lord in their lives to see them become young men (laborers in the Kingdom of God). It seems that as Jesus preached the gospel of the Kingdom, He always called men to the next level—loving and serving God. In Matthew 9, as Jesus was moved deeply with compassion for the needs of all the people, He said, "The harvest truly is plentiful, but the laborers are few. Therefore pray the Lord of the harvest to send out laborers into His harvest" (Matthew 9:37–38 NKJV). Jesus is passionate about having workers in the world. This is our next goal in making disciples.

Important Factors in This Stage of the Discipleship Process:

Grounding in the Faith: They are no longer to be little baby Christians. We must ground them in the Kingdom of God in the following areas:

- *Kingdom Values: secret devotion, giving, and living supernaturally*

- *Kingdom Character: righteousness, peace, joy, love, servanthood, humility, and boldness*

- *Knowledge and Faith in Christ: Who is the Father? Who is Jesus Christ? What did He accomplish for us all at the Cross? Who is the Spirit and how do we walk with Him? What does it mean to be a son and to live with His inheritance?*

The Attitudes of a Servant of Jesus: Here are some basic attitudes that must be developed in the life of a servant of Jesus: a servant's spirit, a heart for people, a passion to multiply, a willingness to volunteer, and a concern for the lost.

The Call of the Great Commission: As we disciple those that Jesus brings into our lives, we must share the wonderful call of the Great Commission from the very beginning—the God of heaven desires to use us to work together with Him to change the world.

The Need for Bringing Inner Healing and Deliverance: As discussed earlier, when people come to us, they are often broken and wounded in many areas of life. In the fathering and mothering process, we must be willing and able to get very involved in these "messy" areas of life. We will often need to lead them through forgiving others, the healing of wounded hearts, the breaking of strongholds created by lies they have believed about themselves and others, and often we must be ready to lead them through deliverance from the powers of darkness.

Young Men: Ministering to Laborers: The Ministry of Discovering and Empowering

Once our spiritual sons and daughters begin to serve God and others in basic ministry, our next goal should be to discover the ministry and leadership gifts and abilities within them. When people become committed to multiplication—that is, to give their lives to make disciples of Jesus—they have entered the realm of leadership. Some can lead a handful of people well, while others are gifted at leading many, but nearly every person committed to Christ can lead some.

Great Commission Ministry Skills: We must seek to develop in those we disciple both deep conviction and heartfelt motivation toward Jesus's call to serve. In addition, we must see that they are equipped for basic ministry. For instance, at this stage of growth, they should have:

- *The ability to share their testimony.*

- *The ability to share the gospel.*

- *Practical service in congregational meetings.*

- *Praying for the sick and casting out demons.*

- *A lifestyle of intercession and prayer.*

Making Disciples: By this stage of growth, the believer should be discipling others. What we or others have done for them previously, they should begin to do for another. They are not a disciple of Jesus until they are discipling others.

Discovery of Their Personal Gifts and Ministries: We must remember in this process that we are not creating ministry robots. Every person is an individual with special God-given gifts, abilities, and callings. They are not ultimately even our disciples or spiritual children, but disciples of Jesus and sons of God the Father. He has a specific will for each person in His service, and as good spiritual parents, we are to help them discover and develop what God has placed within them. Because of this, we have to, like parents in the natural, go on a journey of discovery with them to their unique place and calling in Him.

APPLICATION:

Using the list you created earlier, consider each person and what strategy/practical steps you might use while discipling them so that they will grow into the next stage of maturity.

Chapter Seventeen

PRACTICAL PRINCIPLES OF FATHERING

Raising up mature sons and daughters of God is one of the biggest needs in the world today, and God has given us a pattern in the Scriptures of how and what to do. I want to end this booklet by giving you some of the very practical principles we've employed over the last 25 years. I hope they serve and guide you as well as they have us.

If we accept His challenge to rise up as fathers and mothers to the emerging generations, many lives will be changed (especially ours), and a whole new lineage of laborers is going to be prepared for work in God's field. It is time to begin the work but first, let's explore these principles to guide us in the process.

Foundational Principle: I Cannot Make What I Am Not! The foundation I must work from as I begin to think about making disciples and developing mature sons and daughters is that I cannot make what I am not. If I am not a disciple of Jesus, first and foremost, I cannot make others!

1. CHOOSING WHOM TO INVEST IN

As you begin a life of discipling others, the first step is choosing whom to disciple or father. Don't make this process too difficult. Some people teach that only the father chooses, but I don't believe that this can be backed up biblically. Jesus did choose many of His disciples, but several other times, we see people come to Him and say that they want to follow Him. Here are some helpful things to consider when choosing whom you will invest in:

- *Look for hunger and availability.*

- *Look for those who are teachable.*

- *Look for potential (this does not always have to be the criteria though).*

- *Who is in your life already?*

- *The relationship should be somewhat mutual in feelings. "I want to help you, and you want to grow."*

2. BE INTENTIONAL YET RELATIONAL

Here are some practical things that we've learned about being both intentional and relational at the same time:

- *Don't be accidental; be intentional—you choose to initiate the process. Jesus didn't just hope something happened; He acted deliberately and consistently in the lives of His disciples. Paul was the same way. We see him regularly with groups of men; he is mentoring and training for life and work in Christ. How should you meet? In a small group and/or one-on-one. How often should you meet? That depends upon the group. A sample one hour small-group meeting might look something like this: talk about life for 20 minutes, planned input for 30 minutes, and praying together for 10 minutes.*

- *Keep it relational—be friends. "You are my friends if you do what I command you" (John 15:14 ESV). Act like a father or mother: "To Timothy, my beloved son: Grace, mercy and peace from God the Father and Christ Jesus our Lord" (2 Timothy 1:2 NASB). Practice relational living: "Having thus a fond affection for you, we were well-pleased to impart to you not only the gospel of God but also our own lives, because you had become very dear to us" (1 Thessalonians 2:8 NAS 1977).*

- *The Open Home Principle. As Callie and I branched into the lives of fathering and mothering many years ago, we developed the Open Home Principle. We opened our home most nights each week, and those we were investing in just joined in with what our family was doing. We didn't push our kids aside and say, "Now we have important Kingdom work to do kids, go along and play so Mommy and I can . . . " Those who came to our homes just jumped right into whatever we were doing at that moment. Open your home to those you are ministering to and have meals together. Let them see your parenting and marriage, your character, and your life. The difference between students and sons is here.*

- *Plan trips together—vacations, fun times, etc.*

- *Above all, don't turn people into your projects; make them your friends.*

3. DO IT YOUR WAY

Discipleship must fit your lifestyle. No two families or parents in the natural are the same, and that is true of spiritual parents and families as well. Two families can take the same principles and apply them, but the application will look very different and unique in every case. The life of fathering and mothering should flow out of your own personality and gifts. If someone is a teacher, then teaching will be very prominent in the process. If someone is a server, then serving will be a major element. Allow God to show you your unique way, and do not allow yourself to get put into a religious box.

4. LEARN TO ASK QUESTIONS AND LISTEN

How is your relationship with Jesus? What are you doing to grow?

How is your relationship with your spouse? With your kids?

What have you been doing to minister to others this week?

Have your thoughts been pure? What are your biggest

struggles?

How can I help you the most right now?

In what ways have you been stepping out in faith?

Are you serving others?

Have you shared Jesus with anyone lately?

5. TAKE THEM WITH YOU AS YOU MINISTER

Jesus invested in others by taking them with Him in His ministry journey, letting them both see and do alongside Him. As you take them with you, use the following guidelines: Let them see you in action and ask questions along the way; give them a level of responsibility that stretches, but does not overwhelm; let them minister, even when you can do it better; give them positive and constructive feedback; encourage like crazy! Here are some good follow-up questions after ministry situations: What did you do well? What can you do better? What might you do differently next time?

6. SPEAK THE TRUTH IN LOVE

One of the big errors I personally made many times was that I tried so much to be a friend that I didn't confront. Don't do that! Don't be afraid to confront others you are mentoring along their journey. As your relationship with the person you are discipling develops, you will see character problems, sins, and other things that must be addressed (see Proverbs 3:11–12; 12:1; 17:10; 19:20; 22:6). A good parent brings loving discipline and correction into the lives of their sons and daughters. Remember, timing is everything. People change much faster when they see the problem within themselves first. Give God a bit of time, pray for them, and ask the Lord to begin the work first. Then move forward when He directs. When you do bring the moment of confrontation, make sure your heart is to bring blessing and wholeness, not judgment or criticism.

7. DON'T BUILD OVERDEPENDENCY UPON YOU

Don't be a substitute for Jesus or the Word of God. Allow them to seek out for themselves things they need to learn from Him. Remember, God is the teacher, and they belong to Him. In John 1:35–37, John the Baptist is standing with two of his disciples; he points them to Jesus, and they leave John and follow Jesus. This is the goal of our discipling. People following Jesus! Here are some keys to this principle:

- *Don't make decisions for them.*

- *Allow them to fall and fail at times.*

- *Encourage them to seek ministry from others. Even if God allows you to have a primary role in discipling another, remember that they need much more than you for their fulfillment. Watch out for ownership or jealousy of others in your heart.*

8. BE WILLING FOR THE RELATIONSHIP TO CHANGE AND RELEASE THEM TO GO

As parents in the natural world, when our children become grown, we don't expect them to stay in our homes. Josiah is 32 years old at the time of this writing, Bethany is 29, and Hannah is 25. They are all married and man, am I glad they grew up and left home! Wouldn't it be just a little bit strange if they still all lived with us, and we treated them like we did 20 years ago, and they never matured? The secret is, with maturity comes change. In the same way, we don't raise up spiritual sons just to carry out our vision and stay by our side. Some may serve long term in our lives or ministries, but others will develop a vision of their own. Shouldn't we help them get out there and succeed?

One reason many who disciple, father and mother, don't want the relationship to change is that THEY have become dependent upon the one they are mentoring. Don't become unhealthily dependent on them either. You must release your disciples, spiritual sons and daughters, to fulfill their destiny in God. Some of them will achieve more than you, others will do things very differently from you, but be willing to allow God to form His image and plan in them, not yours. When the time comes, make it easy for them to leave. You may even need to push them out at times. But after releasing them, be there for them when they need you.

9. GET READY TO BE WOUNDED

The life of being a father or mother is a life that has scars; get ready to get hurt a few times along the way. Be sure of this if you give your life to raise up sons in the faith, you will get hurt—quite a few times, in many ways—sometimes hurt very badly. This is the nature of close relationships—when we get close to people, we become vulnerable.

- *Jesus had His Judas. How must have the Son of Man felt when Judas betrayed Him with a kiss only a few hours after dipping bread together in the same bowl? And how much pain must Jesus have felt as he watched 10 others of His closest friends deserted Him a few moments later?*

- *Barnabas must have been cut to the heart when the one he raised up in the Lord, Paul, had a sharp disagreement with him and left his side only to open his own ministry without him.*

- *Paul experienced it many times. Listen to his words in 2 Timothy 4:10 (NASB), "for Demas, having loved this present world, has deserted me and gone to Thessalonica."*

Here's the bottom line—IT'S WORTH IT. It's worth the pain of the journey to see His life formed and matured in sons and daughters. Don't give up when pain finds its way to your door.

10. ENCOURAGE THEM LIKE CRAZY

The final principle is simple, speak life constantly, praising them daily. Declare to them the dreams and visions you see ahead for them. Be their greatest cheerleader. Become a true Barnabas—a Son of Encouragement.

Above all, as you move into this exciting adventure of living as a spiritual father or mother, always remember that there is no secret formula. It's just a lot of love and hard work in the lives of others.

APPLICATION:

Which of these principles is already operating in your life? Which are not, and you need to grow in? What do you expect to happen in the next few years as you apply these principles in the lives of others? Discuss what it would look like (actually write out the picture you describe) in a local church and a region if these principles were to be applied and lived out.

IT'S TIME TO RUN

Callie, my wife, is not really a runner, but years ago, she decided she would begin to run half marathons. That's a little over 13 miles or 21 kilometers. Wow, that seemed like such an uphill battle when she first began. She trained, she ran, she exercised, and she dreamed of running this big race. Month after month of talking, training, running, and then more talking, training, and much more running, the time finally arrived, for she <u>had to choose to enter the race and run.</u> All the training meant nothing unless she entered the race. All the running had some benefit to her, but it would never have the full benefit it was intended unless she entered the race and ran.

I'll never forget the day of her first half marathon. It was a cold, rainy December day in Dallas, Texas, and she had injured her knee about 10 days prior. We didn't know if she could do it. I met her at five different spots throughout the race as both fatigue and pain called to her to pull off the road and quit along the way. The last half mile or so, I could run beside her. I was just there saying, "Just one more step. You can do it. Keep your legs moving. You can finish. Come on babe, one more step." Then she rounded the last corner, and there were about 400 meters to go. The giant professional basketball arena was the finish line, and it loomed large on the horizon; she could see the finish. That street was lined, with perhaps 10,000 people, who called her name, "Callie, you can do it. Come on Callie you're doing great. Finish strong Callie." As she heard that "great cloud of witnesses" calling her name, she found new strength and finished well. As she crossed the finish line, the great runners who had finished ahead of her placed a blanket around her and gave her water. Then the master of the race placed a medal around her neck and said, "Well done, young lady. Please join me in the great banquet party in the basketball coliseum." Callie replied, "Can my husband come with me?" "Oh no, it's only for those who have run my race and finished the course. Come and celebrate the race with me."

I've never forgotten that day. It is indelibly stuck in my spirit, for that's so much like our lives in the Kingdom of God. But especially in the life of fathering and mothering, we get no reward for learning things, talking, and training. There is only a reward if we run. It's time to enter this great race and run! Along the way of a life of giving yourself to raise up and mature the emerging generations, many things will call to you along the way to quit, you'll hear the voice of fatigue, pain, and countless other things, but just keep running.

And one day, we will turn that corner and begin to glimpse our finish line with the great cloud of heaven's witnesses shouting our name, "You can do it. Just one more young man, one more young lady. Give your life away for one more. You can do it. Come on. Finish this race of the Father/Son Paradigm!" Then, we will cross the line and see Him. We will see the Lord Himself, and what more precious thing could we bring to Him than many mature sons and daughters unto His Father? And at that moment, He will place His heavenly reward upon us and say, "My son, My daughter, please join Me in the wedding feast of the Lamb, for it's reserved for those who have entered My race and finished the course. It's time to celebrate! We've won!"

IT'S TIME TO RUN!

ENDNOTES

1. Comiskey, J. (2014, May 30). The Cry for Spiritual Fathers and Mothers. Retrieved from https://churchleaders.com/smallgroups/small-group-blogs/174824-the-cry-for-spiritual-fathers-and-mothers.html

2. Sanchez, C. (2017, June 18). Poverty, Dropouts, Pregnancy, Suicide: What The Numbers Say About Fatherless Kids. Retrieved from https://www.npr.org/sections/ed/2017/06/18/533062607/poverty-dropouts-pregnancy-suicide-what-the-numbers-say-about-fatherless-kids

3. Teachman, J. (n.d.). The Childhood Living Arrangements of Children and the Characteristics of Their Marriages - Jay D. Teachman, 2004. Retrieved from https://journals.sagepub.com/doi/abs/10.1177/0192513X03255346?journalCode=jfia

4. Kirchheimer, S. (2003, January 23). Single-Parent Homes Increase Risk of Child Suicide. Retrieved from https://www.webmd.com/baby/news/20030123/absent-parent-doubles-child-suicide-risk

ABOUT PREPARE INTERNATIONAL

Prepare International is a group of co-laborers from around the world who have a burning desire to see the Kingdom, to enter the Kingdom, to fully express the Kingdom, and to help others do the same in every sector of life today in the nations of the earth.

We have established Biblical training schools in many nations and trained in many other arenas seeing a mighty body of followers growing for the glory of Christ. The Kingdom of God is being rediscovered and is emerging in churches, businesses, industry, education, but above all in homes and the hearts of men.

We are based in Lubbock, Texas but have co-workers and team members in 20+ nations of the earth. You can find out more about us at:

www.pinations.org

For more information about Prepare International, please write us at:

PO Box 53729
Lubbock, TX 79413 USA
office@prepareinternational.org